HOW TO
HANG A PICTURE

HOW TO HANG A PICTURE. Copyright © 2013 by Jay Sacher
and Suzanne LaGasa.
Foreword copyright © 2013 by Anh-Minh Le.
All rights reserved. Printed in China. For information, address
St. Martin's Press, 175 Fifth Avenue, New York, N.Y. 10010.

www.stmartins.com

Illustrations by Jay Sacher
Design by Suzanne LaGasa

The Library of Congress Cataloging-in-Publication Data is
available upon request

ISBN 978-1-250-03603-2 (paper over board)
ISBN 978-1-250-03604-9 (e-book)

St. Martin's Griffin books may be purchased for educational,
business, or promotional use. For information on bulk
purchases, please contact Macmillan Corporate and Premium
Sales Department at 1-800-221-7945, extension 5442, or write
specialmarkets@macmillan.com.

First Edition: November 2013

10 9 8 7 6 5 4 3 2 1

HOW TO
HANG A PICTURE

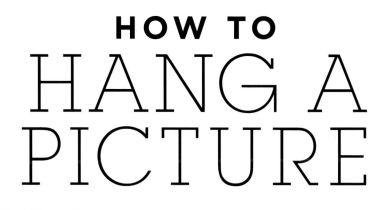

AND OTHER ESSENTIAL LESSONS
FOR THE STYLISH HOME

JAY SACHER and
SUZANNE LaGASA

Foreword by
ANH-MINH LE

St. Martin's Griffin 〽 *New York*

CONTENTS

FOREWORD

AS A FREELANCE WRITER AND MAGAZINE EDITOR, I've interviewed scores of homeowners over the years. No matter what the size, interior style, or locale of their abode, one of the things I most enjoy learning about is the art on the walls. The narrative behind a painting, print, or photograph can be fascinating—whether it is a family heirloom, travel souvenir, work of a friend, or is salvaged from the street. For me, these tend to be the elements that make a home unique and a true reflection of its inhabitants.

At *Anthology,* we receive a lot of scouting images of residences to consider for publication. The more art I see in a space, the more stories I imagine being able to extract from the homeowner and subsequently share with readers. But I have a confession to make: In my own home, I'm often at a loss on how to display art. Regardless of how much I analyze a picture of a seemingly perfect salon-style wall, I can't quite translate the look and feel into my own interior. I find the process of hanging art rather daunting, from start to finish.

How do I choose the mat and frame and glass for this piece? Maybe I should consider a shadow box? What if I hang this painting above the bench and people accidentally rest their heads against it? How do I figure out the hanging mechanism for this very heavy piece? What's the best way to arrange these five things together? Would a single paint color or wallpaper work as the backdrop to this art? Do I need a unifying theme or palette for a grouping? Is there any chance I'm going to hit a pipe if I hammer this nail into the wall?

The list of questions is endless! (That last scenario with the burst pipe actually did happen to a friend of mine.) Sure, there are some walls in my home that, after five years, are finally adorned with art. But in most cases, I agonized over the frames and placement. And I still have a ways to go in the art department. For instance, if you open the built-in cabinet in my living room, you'll find a variety of prints—still in their protective envelopes, waiting to be displayed. In my bedroom, there are a couple of works on the floor, leaning against the wall rather than gracing it.

Alas, I think there is hope for me—as well as others in a similar predicament. With *How to Hang a Picture: and Other Essential Lessons for the Stylish Home,* Jay and Suzanne provide a cure for the empty-wall syndrome that afflicts so many of us. Reading this book is like having a personal consultant guide you through every step of the display process, including answering many of the questions that have crossed my mind.

I'm convinced that if this book existed when I moved into my current house, the artwork wouldn't have been one of the last decor matters to be addressed. Better late than never, though, right?

Anh-Minh Le, Editor in Chief
***ANTHOLOGY* MAGAZINE**

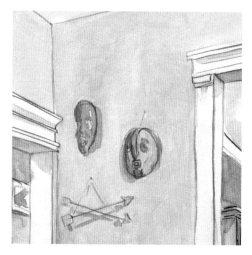

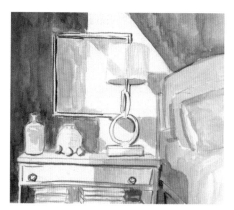

WHERE

SOME THINGS IN LIFE ARE EASY. Some things just *seem* easy. Consider brewing a pot of coffee, or tying a Windsor knot. These are simple acts, the kinds of things people do everyday. There's nothing inherently difficult in the processes behind them, but the fact is that some people do indeed do them better than others. Why is that, exactly? Luck? Skill? Better materials? More practice?

So it is with the seemingly simple act of hanging a picture on a wall. Art on the wall is a tricky thing—it satisfies many, and sometimes contradictory, needs. Is it just a pretty thing on the wall, or is it something greater and grander? In a museum or at a gallery, your role as a visitor is clear: You're to focus your attention on the great works on the wall. You're to experience the work, concentrating and enveloping yourself. Waiting, as Tom Wolfe says, "for something to radiate directly from the paintings on these invariably pure white walls, in this room, in this moment, into [your] own optic chiasma." But what about art in your kitchen? Or your study? How much attention do you need to give to that painting on your wall while you're doing your taxes or feeding your cat? Is it just decor to be glanced at out of the corner of your eye, or is it something more?

Charles Baudelaire once said that art should "contain an element of the eternal and an element of the transitory." If we're going to be high-minded about it, providing solutions to that conflict is what this book is about. Art should transport us and enlighten us, but, as a part of one's home, it needs to look good on purely aesthetic grounds, it needs to match the wallpaper, so to speak. An integral part of marrying art to the home (or the office, or the studio) is in how that art is displayed. How do you hang a picture and make it look good both as a piece of art and as decor? Like many simple acts, there's a science at work in hanging art that, when completed with care and consideration, can become a hallmark of personal style. This little book is your mechanical spec sheet for that process.

There is no single *right* way to hang a picture. There are however, plenty of *wrong* ways. *How to Hang a Picture* is designed to help you develop a sense of what's right for your own personal style. It's also a nuts-and-bolts how-to manual. We approached the subject as novices would—what would you need to know if you had no framework on which to base your visual or technical judgments? Just as a grammarian might parse the lines of a poem, we pulled apart the simple act of hanging a picture to detail the undercarriage of aesthetic principles and technical skill that compose this most basic aspect of adorning your home.

We began by speaking with the experts. From gallery owners and professional art curators, to interior designers and building contractors, to artists and photographers themselves—we wanted to know what they practice when hanging art. The goal was to map out what works the best *and looks the best* for the least amount of money. Straightaway, we discovered that there are basic principles to follow when hanging art on your wall, and there are plenty of tips and tricks that can help you with everything from DIY framing to securing heavy art on a wall. Along with the technical know-how we've compiled, we reached out to our friends and colleagues, imploring them to send us photos of walls they adore (in their home or elsewhere), or to send us their personal design solutions for hanging art in tricky spaces, from the narrow hallway to the brick-walled city studio. The watercolor illustrations in the book are inspired by these real homes and real spaces around the world—our hope is that by seeing how other people have utilized the basic know-how we've compiled in this book (or how they've completely avoided "the rules"), you'll be inspired to create your own unique spaces.

The book is divided into four sections. The first section details the act of planning. We provide you with a variety of loose, but very important, aesthetic guideposts. The goal isn't to make you a rigid adherent to a bland set of rules, but instead to help you inform your own personal vision with basic principles that are wielded by artists, curators, and designers everywhere.

The second section is straight-up hammer, nails, drills, and screws. Now that you know where you'd like to hang your art, we make sure you won't ruin your walls as you do so. Whether you rent or own, whether you have antique lath-and-plaster walls or modern drywall, there's no sense in using the wrong tools in the wrong places. With help from the charts, how-to illustrations, and simple instructions in this section, you should be able to approach any wall and accomplish any design solution regardless of your living space.

In the third section, we discuss framing art. We start with everyone's big issue with framing: It's expensive. Whether you buy the tools and learn how to do it all yourself, or take your art to a professional framer, you're going to spend more money than you'd like. The only real solution to the issue of cost is to follow a strategy expounded by a new generation of DIY style mavens that's best described as a mix-match ethos. For every kind of art—from oil paintings on canvas to silkscreened prints—and all the resources in your designer's toolbox (from the nuts and bolts of lighting to the tried-and-true philosophies behind color theory), we showcase various ways to get creative without spending too much money and ensure that the art on your walls is both considered and beautiful.

In the fourth section, we discuss a few easily overlooked aspects of art display: lighting and shelving. Shelves, from bookcases to dedicated picture ledges, can round out a wall's composition and transform a space. As for lighting, well—sometimes you have too much, sometimes too little—we'll share some basic insights on making the most of both natural and man-made light sources to help magnify the beauty of the artwork.

This book is meant to inform and inspire. The art on your wall can be whatever you want it to be: It can recede calmly into the background or be a joyous expression of personal taste. It can be serious or whimsical or nostalgic or shocking. It will, however, be something you look at and sit with quite often, every day. It deserves to be given thought and care. We hope our book will help you hang pictures happily, with intention and style.

Centering your art at eye level is a key component to a well-planned wall.

FIFTY-SEVEN INCHES

It's the most basic of all wall-hanging questions: Where will you hang your art? On the surface, it seems like a fairly straightforward line of inquiry. Art on a wall is not a foreign notion to any of us—we've all seen it—we all know what it looks like and we have a general sense that, unless we're trying to make some sort of particular artistic statement, it shouldn't be hung too high or too low on the wall. It seems like we should know what to do: Find the space on the wall where it looks good to the eye, mark off a spot for the nail, and hammer away. And it really is almost that simple— almost. But hanging a picture is guided by basic principles that can't be overlooked.

For a parallel idea, consider the bowline knot—the "king of knots," used for a variety of purposes and integral to sailing. It's a simple knot, taught to children with the old tale of a rabbit coming out of its hole and around a tree and hopping back into its hole again. The greatness of the bowline is that it's as effective as it is simple, and while you can tie a bowline without comprehending why it holds so well, the mechanics of the bowline knot are guided by notions of geometry and resistance that are essential for a sailor to understand. Likewise, hanging art is an aesthetic exercise, and aesthetically speaking, there are essential mechanics at work when you put something up on a wall for people to look at—if you examine those mechanics, a few basic principles become evident. It's these principles that we will showcase as the "rules" of hanging art.

Think of adorning your walls as a sort of language, and the "rules" of hanging are basically its grammar. Once you learn the rules, you can start speaking the language with style. You don't have to follow all the rules all the time, but they're a great place for the novice to start. The best thing about the rules is that *they always work*. If you take nothing else away from this book, pay close attention to the following how-to and you will have a fail-safe design solution in your back pocket.

Let's suppose that you have a ready-to-hang piece of art and a blank wall in front of you—it's time to decide where you will hang your piece. Taking aside all considerations of, let's say, a large piece of furniture, or window moldings or fireplace mantels or anything else that might be "in the way," the most elegant solution, the one that any designer will use as a jumping-off point, is that your art should be hung at eye level.

This is common sense, but it's surprising how often it's overlooked. It's been said that any piece of art should look good from twelve feet away and twelve inches away—hanging art at eye level helps make that maxim a reality. It's where our eye wants to look. This is a central tenet of graphic design. If you're about to place an image on a blank page, you want that image to be what is known as "optically centered." If it's too low, the viewer tends to interpret the image as falling off the page, and if it's too high, our mind imagines the image as rushing upward away from us. An optically centered image is one that is not at the dead center of the page, but one that corresponds to the viewer's ideal sight line (in the case of a page, this is usually slightly above the actual "center" of the page).

This same sort of rule applies to a wall. People often assume that for the sake of symmetry, art should be hung at the dead center of a wall. But dead center on a wall is more often than not an odd and awkward height when compared with one's sightlines.

What this all means is simple: The exact center of your art should be hung at roughly fifty-seven inches height. Fifty-seven inches—give or take an inch or two—is about the average sightline for a human being. When planning the design of a blank wall, it's a great place to begin—creating an anchor for the viewer's sight. This rule becomes especially useful when you are hanging a variety of pictures of varying sizes in the same room. As you plan the wall, a system of weights and balances naturally reveals itself. You have several pieces of art, all different sizes, spread across a wall, and with their centers at fifty-seven inches, they are all perfectly poised for

TOOLS:
Measuring tape
Soft pencil

Optional:
Ball of string
Ruler
Painter's tape

viewing and a compliment to the room it-self. Now that you know why, here's how:

Once you've chosen the basic area on the wall from which you'd like to hang your piece, you'll need to mark off the point where the center of your art will sit. This is easily done with a measuring tape and a soft pencil. If you haven't al-ready done so, now would be a good time to eyeball how the art actually looks in this space by having a friend hold it up roughly in position as you take a look. Keep in mind that generally speaking, the bottom of your art should never be closer than eight inches to the top of a couch or chair. This is less an aesthetic principle than a practical one, you don't want sitters to lean back and touch the art by accident. *(fig. 1)*

Next, locate the exact center of your art. Begin by turning your art over and use your measuring tape (or ruler, if the art is smaller) to measure along its bot-tom edge. Mark the center of that mea-surement with your pencil as close to the frame or edge of the art as possible. Mark off the corresponding measurement along its top edge (that is, if your art is twenty inches wide, you should make a hash mark at the ten-inch mark along its bottom and the top).

Repeat this step for the opposing length of the art, leaving you with four hash marks at the outer centers of your art. *(fig. 2)*

Using your ruler or measuring tape, connect the hash marks with a light pen-cil line; where the lines cross signifies the center of your art. *(fig. 3)* If you cannot

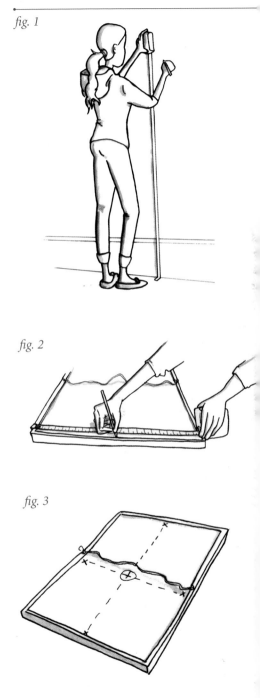

fig. 1

fig. 2

fig. 3

fig. 4 and 5

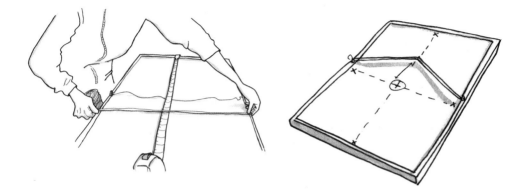

mark up the backside of your art, an alternative method is to lay your measuring tape or ruler down along one of the set of hashes (the up-down axis, say) and lay a string along the opposite axis. Mark off the center with a small piece of removable painter's tape. *(fig. 4)*

You now have two points, one on the wall and one on the back of your art, that need to match up once the item is hung. Depending on how the art will be fastened to the wall, you may need to make a few adjustments to know where to put the nail. (For information on choosing wall fasteners that are right for your wall and your art, see section How)

In many cases, framed art will be hung from a wire. You'll need to determine the amount of play that exists between the wire and the center of the art. Simply "hang" the wire from your index finger, pulling the wire taut. Position the art as straight as possible. Measure the distance from the center of the art to your finger. *(fig. 5)*

Similarly, if your picture has hooks embedded in it or you are using another hanging method, you need to measure the point from where the hooks will fasten to the wall to the center point of the art. Add that extra measurement to your fifty-seven-inch mark on the wall, and you can then mark off exactly where you should affix your wall fastener or picture hanger. So if the picture wire of your piece hangs taut at three and a half inches, go to the mark you've made on your wall and measure up three and a half inches to reach sixty and a half inches, which is where you will affix your picture hanger.

Two equally sized pieces hung at eye level. *Lisa Wong Jackson and Nick Jackson, Berkeley, CA.*

The graphic quality of these shipping-container photographs combine with their placement for a compelling display. *Steven Wade, Lakewood, OH.*

Keep in mind that the fifty-seven-inch rule is the completist's approach to planning out your wall hangings. It is not a hard rule, but it's one that works. For instance, what if, as described earlier, the placement of your couch or an especially tall bureau competes too much or is too close to art hung at eye level? There's no crime in shifting your art accordingly. Since the goal is to create a balanced composition, consider the whole piece of furniture you're hanging your art above as part of that composition. The "eight-inch rule" we mention previously is a good guidepost, especially when you're hanging a large single piece above a static object like a bureau or a bookcase, but if you're attempting to hang several pieces of varying sizes, you may want to play with the distances a bit more, hanging a few pieces lower so that they create a bridge between the furniture and the art on the wall. The worst thing you can do is hang a single piece of art too high and perfectly centered over a piece of furniture—it creates a sort of floating effect that is jarring to the viewer. Also consider how the purpose of the furniture might dictate your composition. We've seen many sleek and functional work desks with art hung almost level with the lip of the desk, mirroring the feel of a bulletin board, whereas that same approach probably wouldn't work above a kitchen counter or bathroom sink. Take extra care when placing art above couches or chairs that have their backs to walls. Depending on your couch-reclining habits (or those of your fort-building toddler), eight inches above the top of your couch might be just a tad too low for art if you want to limit errant arms and backs of heads interfering with the art, but you'll need to balance that concern against the visually felonious crime of art hung too high.

CHEAT SHEET

Ideal height for art on wall, centered:

57" - 60"

Ideal distance from bottom edge of art to
top of edge of furniture:

6" - 8"

Ideal distance between pieces of art:

3" - 6"

Like all good design solutions, the fifty-seven-inch "rule" is both elegant and practical. As such, it's a great starting point from which to craft the look of an entire room. Use it as a way to create balance between two pictures that you'd like to pair on a wall, one big, one smaller. If both are hung with their centers at fifty-seven inches, they will both be optically centered, while their disparate sizes work together to create a pleasing tug of war between each other.

The everyday wisdom on the distance between artworks is that each piece should be at least six inches apart. That figure is probably a good visual guide, but shouldn't be considered a hard rule. What you want to avoid is the sense of artworks being piled atop each other or cramped together—whether that means six inches or nine inches or three inches is up to your own personal taste and the look you're hoping to achieve. If you're hanging two objects that are the same size and are meant to pair with each other in a particular way, you might want a different sense of space between the pieces than if it's a more casual arrangement.

While you can hang all your art at fifty-seven inches, if you're planning a wall with more than one piece, you can use the fifty-seven-inch rule for all the pieces on your wall or one: an anchored piece at fifty-seven inches, with a variety of satellite pieces balanced off the central image.

Anchoring one of three pieces at eye level can create optical balance. *Anna Wolf and Mike Perry, Brooklyn, NY.*

This multipurpose living space features a trio of art hung at complementary heights. *Jordan Provost and Jason Wong, Brooklyn, NY.*

The power of a single piece properly hung speaks for itself. *Miranda Dempster and Gus Mckay, New York, NY.*

A grided salon-style wall. *Miranda Dempster and Gus McKay, New York, NY.*

THE
SALON

Once you start thinking about the aesthetics of hanging art, it becomes kind of hard to stop. Pictures on the wall are everywhere. Every café and restaurant, every corporate headquarters and government office, and most every home. Armed with the fifty-seven-inch rule, you start to notice things, with the most common mistake being that people tend to hang their art too high in an effort to "center" their art on the wall or not have it interfere with furniture.

Of course, there are plenty of ways and reasons to hang art at any height you please, not the least of which being that following a rule just because it's a rule is generally a silly thing to do. However, we like the fifty-seven-inch rule for its simplicity and versatility—even when they "break it," adherents of its versatility are aware of why they're breaking it. One very good reason to break the rule is that you have too much art to hang for the amount of wall you possess. Thus was born the "salon style" of hanging.

The "salon" to which this style refers was the Paris Salon of the nineteenth century, also known by its more formal title, "The Exhibition of Living Artists." The annual exhibition was named after the Salon Carré (the square room) of the Louvre, where the exhibition was originally held, beginning in 1673. In 1855, the Salon moved to the Palais des Champs-Elysées, a massive cast-iron exhibition hall that, along with the affordable ticket price, allowed some 23,000 people a day to view the exhibition during its annual six-week run.

The Salon was often a make-or-break proposition for aspiring artists—thousands of works were submitted each year, with about a fifty-fifty chance of an artist making the grade. Those that weren't had the indignity of the underside of their canvases being stamped with a red "r," for "refusé." As tastes in contemporary art changed, an alternate exhibition, the Salon des Refusés (featuring work cast out of the Salon) came to herald the vanguard of Impressionism, featuring works by Edouard Manet, James MacNeil Whistler, and others. The artworks that made it into the official Salon were hung for the public in an epic floor-to-ceiling display—an impressive and massive array of canvas from across France. Of interest to our inquiry, art that was unanimously voted in by the notoriously fickle and political judging committee was granted the opportunity to be hung "on the line," meaning they would be placed on the wall at the most visually pleasing sightline.

It is from this potboiler of an art show that we arrive at modern salon-style hanging—which basically means large clusters of art hung at varying heights on one wall. The benefits of a salon wall are obvious—it's a visual treat for the viewer and a great way to overcome space restrictions to showcase art that you otherwise wouldn't be able to hang.

PLANNING A SALON-STYLE WALL

Sometimes you have an instant vision for how to arrange the art on your wall. No planning necessary: *That* has to go *there*. With a salon-style wall, it's a little harder to envision how multiple items will look on your wall, so planning can be very helpful, unless you have fifteen or so friends willing to hold art in place while you survey the scene from afar.

An easy option for planning a salon wall requires little more than some butcher paper, a measuring tape, a pencil, and some painter's tape.

First, measure out the basic wall area you'll be filling with art. You can eyeball it or you can choose to be incredibly exact—it depends on the space you're trying to fill. (If, say, you are planning a wall where fixtures such as moldings, mantels, or other obstacles might interfere with your art, it pays to take extra care with your measuring tape.)

Then, on an open area of floor, lay out a few sheets of butcher paper that correspond to the size of your wall space. If you don't have butcher paper, any large sheets of paper will do, even the backs of disused wrapping paper. Tape the backs of the paper to fit them together. As noted, mark off on the butcher paper the locations of any obstacles on the wall (thermostat, light switches, and so on).

Now, gather the art that you plan to hang and begin arranging it on the paper. (*fig. 1*) While (as always) there is no right and wrong way to plan your wall, if you are looking for guideposts, one option is to make sure that one or more "anchor" pieces that you want to showcase are hung with their centers at eye level—follow the same fifty-seven-inch rule that you learned in the section Fifty-seven Inches.

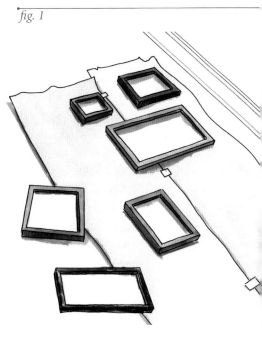

fig. 1

Usually, you'd want between three and six inches of space between each piece of art, but you can have less or more to suit your arrangement (although we've seen it done now and then, we'd advise against creating a cluster of art where the frames of corresponding pieces touch each other—it tends to look cramped and crowded and oddly "unplanned").

The classic salon-style wall is one that contains art of all sizes staggered across a wall with no even edges. Some pieces might be almost flush with the edge of a wall, others a few inches in. However, as you'll see from the examples in this chapter, you can arrange a cluster of art with even rows or a more checkerboard approach. Keep in mind that if you do decide to create a symmetrical arrangement, it pays to be both exact and consistent with your measurements and planning—when an objective eye is viewing your final product, it will be drawn to any break in the symmetry.

fig. 2

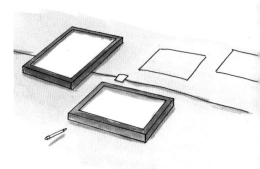

Once you have an arrangement that you are happy with, trace the outer edges of each piece of art onto the butcher paper. *(fig. 2)* This is also a good time to determine where you'll eventually have to affix your art to the wall to achieve this arrangement: if any of your pieces have hanging wire with a lot of play in it, mark off on the butcher paper how much above the art's center you will need to nail to accommodate the play of the wire.

Salon-style walls can run floor to ceiling or in a band across a wide wall, as in this example.

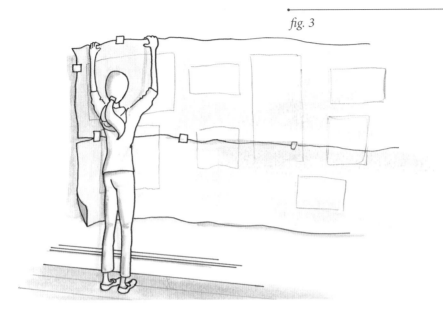

fig. 3

Now it's time to test your arrangement. Remove your art from the paper, and, using tape, hang the entire traced wall up in place. *(fig. 3)* If you're happy with how it looks, you're ready to start hanging, if not, you can adjust the arrangement.

Transferring your plan to the wall takes a little patience and careful measurement—we're going to provide a sort of Type-A way of achieving it, but you can go a little looser if you're confident about how your wall looks. First make sure that the heights of your hanging "paper gallery" are exactly where you want them to be. Do you have an anchor piece hung at eye level? Are there obstructions from furniture or light switches? Is the distance between each space even or symmetrical?

Now, if you haven't already marked off on the paper where you need to affix your hangers to the wall, you can do it piece by piece—lift your art and measure out exactly where the picture hanger you'll be using needs to be placed (pull picture wire taut, make sure D rings or other hardware are positioned correctly), and then transfer those measurements to your hanging paper gallery.

From this point, it's easy to hang your art directly over the paper gallery. Try to work from one side to the other in order so you can see the wall come together—and take plenty of breaks to step back and see how the wall looks from afar and from different angles. A classic salon-style wall should be an energetic mix of symmetry and asymmetry—different art styles and sizes should flow from one to another—creating the impression of a jumble without quite being disorganized. One of the

fig. 4

easiest ways to achieve this is to keep the distances between the artworks roughly equal—they might be different shapes and sizes and colors might clash, but the spacing will help with flow. *(fig. 4)*

Once all the art is hung, you can gently cut away and pull out the paper gallery. Be sure to clean your wall once you're done hanging—there's bound to be a few errant handprints and smudges.

An alternate method for hanging a salon-style display is useful if you're a little less sure of your vision for the wall. Once you've laid out your art and traced it onto the paper gallery, you can begin cutting out the traced shapes of the art one by one. Start in the upper left-hand corner—cut out one piece and gently tape it to the wall in the corresponding spot. Once you've transferred your arrangements to the wall, if you're not satisfied with the overall look, you can choose to move the cutouts about like pieces on a game board. Proceed to hang the art after you've reached a final decision on placement.

The salon style, or arrangements inspired by it, ably adapts to a wide variety of spaces and tastes. A stairway or stairwell is a perfect place to display a cascading wall of imagery. Or, an evenly spaced grid of equally sized artwork makes a statement that draws attention to the work—be careful about placing your art too high up on the wall with this approach: it's easy to become both too austere and too precious.

While we are firm believers in letting art be "art," there are times when decorating choices such as color schemes can play a big role in creating an atmosphere for a particular room or art arrangement. A salon-style wall with a color theme can help hold a wide array of art together that might be otherwise quite thematically diverse. A salon color scheme can be something to work toward or against—Do you craft an array of similarly colored pieces, or do you have one "black sheep" stand out to break up the scheme? Do you craft a theme in another manner? All drawings? All photographs? Or perhaps by subject matter? What about using the same kind of frame for each piece? Even a "no theme" wall is still thematic unless you're literally just throwing paintings onto the wall and not looking at where they end up.

The best way to ensure that your salon wall doesn't seem incongruous or jarring or busy is to plan it out (of course), but also to think about the space you're filling. If

A paper sculpture is the centerpiece of this bold salon-style arrangement. *Jim Campbell, Brooklyn, NY.*

Mixed-media wall. *Christine Schmidt and Evan Gross, San Francisco, CA.*

you're creating a salon wall for a long, connecting hallway, consider arranging the imagery so that it flows horizontally from one end of the hallway to the other, rather than in a vertical bunch. If you're filling the multilevel stairway of a home, you want to ensure that the arrangement looks good from both the top and the bottom of the stairs—that it doesn't feel unfinished from either vantage point.

Don't try to compete with furniture or other aspects of the wall, that is, unless you're trying to make a statement. Floor-to-ceiling displays that wrap around and above door frames can be stunning, but you have to be willing to commit—you have to make sure you have enough art to fill the space. Like hitting a baseball, the salon style is all about follow-through.

Another, less intensive way to display multiple art pieces is to use a few well-placed corkboards or pinboards, creating a rotating mood wall of pushpin art, photos, notes, calendars, and photographs. Corkboard is surprisingly expensive, so as an alternate, you can use white foam-core boards and apply them to your wall as panels. Foam-core board, also called foamboard, is a thick amalgamation of polystyrene with layers of paper that can be used for displaying artwork and photographs.

There are a variety of foamboard hangers with metal teeth that embed in the back of the board (from which you then hang the board using screws, nails, or tacks), but you can also drive holes into the corners of the board (craft and art supply stores sell cheap foamboard "drills"). Using the holes to affix the board to the wall with screws or nails will create a cleaner look and a more secure hold.

Pinboards can be anything from a day-to-day office tool to a daily devotional reminder of art and ephemera to inspire you. In our office, we have two pinboards, one featuring a collection of art, mementos, and curious, and its companion, a more straightforward array of hand-drawn calendars, reminders, and work notes.

A truly diverse wall of mixed media, sculpture, hangings, tapestries, and paintings or prints can have a dramatic effect. Certain rooms in the Isabella Stewart Gardner Museum in Boston, Massachusetts, are a classic example of salon displays where every aspect of the room works as a piece of art. Gardner, a nineteenth-century millionaire who was described by a newspaper reporter of the era as a tastemaker who possessed the "the courage of eccentricity," amassed an impressive collection of classic art, all housed in her villa-cum-museum on the edge of Boston's Fen Gardens. Gardner presented the artwork in arrangements that feel intensely personal (rather than in historical or regional context as other museums might), and as much of the art is presented without labels or placards signifying who the artist is, it's easy to get lost in little corners of the collection, happily experiencing the works rather than studying them. A stroll through the halls of the museum can be great inspiration for designing your own art showcase.

Stairwell salon-style hanging. *Laura and Ben DeHaan, Portland, ME.*

A mix of art prints, sketches, and oil paintings. *Sean McCarthy, Brooklyn, NY.*

Colorful wallpaper and eclectic art hold this space together. *Linda and John Meyers, Portland, ME.*

REAL-LIFE
SPACES
AND REAL-LIFE
COLORS

The great thing about art is that it doesn't *really* have to match anything. It's art—it just has to be itself. Even if you're simply hanging family photos, they still possess an emotional power no matter where you put them. Nevertheless, hanging art is an act that a considerate person tends to put some thought into—extra care and insight only help showcase the work and create a space that is inspiring and engaging. We should at least put as much time into where we put art as we do when we determine where we will put our new flat-screen television.

So far, we've given you some very basic planning tools and principles. In this section, we'll lay out the hammer-to-nail kinds of challenges that can often stop people from hanging art plentifully and properly. In the meantime, we need to acknowledge a simple fact: every space is unique. Galleries and museums are wide and bare and white-walled so that nothing distracts the visitor from the art on the wall. But we don't live in galleries, we live in homes that serve a multitude of purposes and must conform to a variety of personal passions and basic needs.

Every home is a design challenge. A narrow hallway, an urban bedroom facing a dark air shaft, a once "grown-up" living room now flooded with a sea of a toddler's toys, odd placements of fixtures or too much clutter or not enough storage space—all of these, and many more issues, can affect how one hangs art.

There are solutions to these challenges, however. Creative people can turn even the most challenging spaces into harmonic and wonderfully lived-in homes, conducive to love, work, and the day-to-day business of life. Well-placed art on the walls might not be the only key to such an endeavor, but it sure doesn't hurt. This chapter details some real-life design challenges for the hanging of art, or how art helped overcome a secondary problem with a space. Along the way, we showcase a variety of ways to hang art that will help you solve your own design challenges and give you a crash course on some basic principles of color, design, display, and decor.

THE POWER OF THE PERSONAL

Not only is every space different, but everyone has different design goals and aesthetics. You know best what you need out of a living space, and how it will fit with your own philosophy. Consider the San Diego–based artist Susie Ghahremani. She approaches art on the walls as an avenue of solace. To Ghahremani, art on display in the home "should be kind of a window to what we love most in our lives, our world, and ourselves." In her case, that means work from a wide variety of friends and colleagues in her community of artists, a mixture of drawings, paintings, and prints. As to how to integrate that into the home she shares with her husband, Ghahremani admits freely that their home is both "very, very, small" and continuously cluttered.

The cluttered home is not a unique problem. Let's face it, outside of the austere modernist pads photographed in the pages of lifestyle magazines, what homes *aren't* cluttered? But no matter where you fall on the clutter scale, you will need to achieve balance between the art on your wall that brings you joy, and the necessary business that needs to get done every day inside your home. Susie's solution is to give the walls "breathing space" by creating art clusters in odd corners here and there, and by letting other, more personal pieces stand free from distracting adornments and speak for themselves. Susie also uses shelves and counter spaces to great effect, which we discuss in more detail in later chapters.

Everyday clutter can also be subdued by mixing high and low, big and small, to create a depth and a sense of scale that might not be achievable otherwise. Hang large art over a mantelpiece or bureau and juxtapose it with a display of miniature art objects, ceramics, or other smaller arrangements on the bureau below the art.

When you get down to it, juxtaposition is the key to displaying art in the home, since a home is a juxtaposition in itself. A home is multipurposed and multifaceted— it means many different things at once. If you try too hard to create the perfect space for viewing art, you end up with a museum rather than a home. Nicola Trezzi, the U.S. editor for the Milan-based magazine *Flash Art* spoke of visiting homes where the owners had collected art in a way (no matter how "correct" or fashionable it might be) that made everything seem as impersonal as "a Chelsea gallery." The mistakes and the marriage of different tastes and styles are the keys to both good art collecting and good art display. "Think about your wall as the plate, and the art on it as your meal," Trezzi says. "You don't want to eat steak with a side of sausages, or a hamburger with a cheesecake." You want decent, edible pairings that please all the senses. In showcasing art, one way to make this happen is by mixing the personal with the professional. A framed silkscreen print can be paired with a child's doodles

An array of art can help bridge transitional spaces to the rest of the home.

Richly colored walls and three-dimensional objects complete this transitional wall space.
Jordan Provost and Jason Wong, Brooklyn, NY.

or a piece of downscale ephemera. This makes for good viewing and helps tell a story. And if your walls tell a story, they will take care of themselves, fitting seamlessly into your home.

COLOR IS A TOOL AND IT'S ON YOUR SIDE

We won't get too hokey in describing the power of color and color themes to change the dynamic of a space. We'll keep it simple: there's a science at work in color theory, and it works.

COLOR THEORY MADE SIMPLE

At some point in high school art class or beyond, you probably made a color wheel. We won't ask you to make another one, but within that wheel are the basics of color theory.

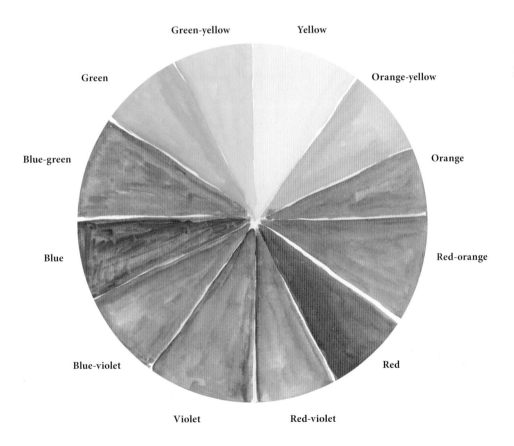

Art placement can help create a breakfast nook out of a wall abutment.

Since experiencing color is subjective, the tenets of color theory, developed over the centuries by artists, scientists, and philosophers, are an intriguing mix of actual fact about how colors work and educated conjecture about how we perceive them. Classical color theory is therefore not an exact science as much as it is a philosophy, but it's a philosophy that talented artists have used to their advantage over the generations.

For our purposes, we'll stick to the basics of how most people perceive colors when those colors interact with one another, and how that can help you plan your display of art. Back to the color wheel: Colors that appear next to each other on the wheel (like blue and blue-green) are known as analogous, and colors that appear opposite each other on the wheel are known as complementary. Classically speaking, analogous colors are thought to construct an emotional response in the viewer since they showcase a tonal range of one color (warm reds or cool blues, for instance), while complementary colors inspire a more visual and immediate reaction by the juxtaposition of oppositions (showcasing those warm reds against cool greens, for instance).

As you plan your wall, think about the visual story you're trying to tell. If you have a large "anchor" piece that is aqua-toned, for instance—one that's already taking up a large portion of wall space—you may not want to draw it out further by pairing it with a work that has strong orange tones (or at the very least, you'd want a neutral-colored frame, like black or white, to help achieve balance). Conversely, you can create a wall of "harmonious adjacents" by displaying a trio of art choices that share the same analogous color scheme (oranges and yellows, or reds and violets, for example).

Of course, in real-life, you're very rarely dealing with two colors, so consider some of these harmonious triads—color combos designed to be a visual feast. (Triads are made by drawing a triangle between three evenly spaced points on the color wheel.)

In painting or graphic design, triads generally have one dominant color, while the remaining two do backup work. This, too, can translate to a wall display.

Red + Yellow + Blue

Red-orange + Yellow-green + Blue-violet

Yellow-orange + Blue-green + Red-violet

We are just barely dipping our toes into the world of color theory—there are also color rectangles, which pair two complementary colors with analogous partners, and split complements, which pair a color with two analogous complements (violet, orange, and green, for instance), and a world more to know and to explore. The basic idea resolves around the notion of complementary and adjacent color harmonies, but it's easy to see how a considered use of color can amplify the power of a wall display.

We asked the artist Sean Greene, whose paintings feature swirling patterns of bold colors, how he and his wife approach hanging art in their home in western Massachusetts. Greene understands that when dealing with art that is primarily driven by bold colors, you need to expect that it will make an impression on the space in which it is displayed. He notes, for instance, that his paintings tend to recede on yellow-toned walls, and that "dulling" the whites of gallery walls slightly toward gray can help focus the viewer's attention on the art, and solely the art. The power of gray as a contrasting element is a tenet of the philosophy of fine-art painting, taken straight from Michel Chevreul's 1855 treatise, "The Principles of Harmony and Contrast of Colours." Primary colors, Chevreul writes, "gain in brilliancy and purity by the proximity of gray." Remember the power of gray when choosing a white paint for your wall, or when choosing a color for a mat—even a subtle shade of gray can do more than the brilliantly white wall we think we want.

Color, therefore, is both a unifier and a divider. When Greene plans a wall (either at home or in a gallery setting), he reminds us that "sometimes, you want to unify the whole atmosphere, in other situations you want to feature an object by contrasting the background or using stronger light." What this means in practical terms is that you should remember your analogous color schemes as a way to blend artwork into your surroundings, and your complementary schemes for making artwork pop off the wall. This is especially important if you're hanging art on walls painted a color other than white. Colors are not set in stone—they will literally look different to the viewer depending on what colors are adjacent to them, and the subjective way in which viewers perceive color in general. A dramatic example of this is called the Bezold effect—named for a nineteenth-century German meteorologist who wrote an elaborate treatise on color. He noted that a single color interspersed with lines of white will look entirely different when the same color is interspersed with lines of black.

FRAME COLOR CHOICE

A quick note on the color and its relation to your frame. Neutral colors (blacks, whites, or wood tones) tend to work best for any kind of artwork, but even then it is important to think about the contrast between your frame and your work. Just as we saw with analogous and complementary colors, the same principle works with frames—you don't want to highlight the frame, you want to highlight the work inside it. So, for

Multiple hangings help hide otherwise unsightly wall fixtures. *Kate Lacey, Brooklyn, NY.*

Elevated shelving and sophisticated art help make this space work for both child and adult.
Lisa Wong Jackson and Nick Jackson, Berkeley, CA.

instance, an image that is predominantly dark—with heavy, thick swatches of somber colors—might not be suited to a white frame, since a bold white frame would be like drawing a bright circle around your art. Just as with clothing, however, black tends to go with just about anything.

MULTIPURPOSE SPACES

Home is where we eat, sleep, commune, work, play, relax, exercise, do our taxes, throw parties, bathe, argue, romance, and laugh. It's multipurpose by its very definition, but as lifestyles change, those mixed needs of space can become more pronounced. Whether you have an office space in your spare bedroom or a child's play area in the living room, art can be used to ease those transitions, and create spaces within spaces.

A corner office "nook" can be complemented with an array of art that sets it apart from the rest of the space—either in tone or in arrangement—perhaps a slim, stacked salon gallery that leads up the wall, or a sole, sober piece that centers the workspace and helps create a sense of focus. A removal of clutter is always a good idea in a work area—keep art and knickknacks on a desk space to a minimum, using shelves or shadow boxes to display your "cubicle" accoutrement.

Children's play areas can be a challenge, especially when you're trying to balance the need to create a welcoming environment for a child without infantilizing your entire home. Consider using furniture just as much as art—a small, child-sized desk instantly makes the ownership of a space clear to child and adult alike. Art can then be hung lower on the wall to match the desk and the sightline of younger eyes. Juxtaposing the child's area with art hung at standard heights or with a more tonal shift of color can help distinguish the "border" between the spaces as well. Another option is to consider wall decals—art studios such as Lorena Siminovich's Petit Collage create a beautiful array of high-quality decals that can be mixed and matched to create attractive compositions—and easily removed to make way for new displays. Or you can always go with a kid-sized corkboard with original art, photos, and fun finds.

BRIDGING THE GAP

Art can also be used to provide a bridge between two spaces, especially useful in homes with open floor plans, or smaller spaces like a studio apartment, where the kitchen might blend into the more general living area. The kitchen chalkboard is an increasingly popular way to both mark off space and create a lovely, aspirational mood board—it makes clear that the kitchen is a space for doing, planning, and prepping. Pair that with more reflective art in the dining area, and you go a long way to creating a new environment (at least philosophically) from scratch.

The dreaded television conundrum. Mere appliance or eyesore?

UNSIGHTLY FIXTURES

Especially in converted spaces, or homes in brick-lined buildings, exposed features like circuit boxes, light switches, and heating pipes can all be a detriment to what we might originally envision as our ideal art display. You can try to cover the offending obstacles, but you'll probably have better luck integrating them into your display. This can be as simple as arranging art around them, or by painting the fixtures the same color as the wall, or (and this might be our favorite) using that wall space to showcase more unusual, three-dimensional objects, or using shelf displays that hide the offending objects. There's also the old slightly meta trick of "framing" a circuit box with an empty frame.

TV PARTY TONIGHT

What to do with the dreaded television? Despite the fact that you might use it to watch a great film now and again, the TV (or the computer screen that doubles as a media player) is basically anti-art. We don't mean this in a political way—it's just that a TV draws you into itself rather than makes you reflect on the surroundings you are in—it's its own picture show, and to be worth it, a TV *needs* to be front and center and easily viewable.

How different creative people deal with this design challenge without ceding to the television the traditional focal point of the "living" room is endlessly fascinating, and could easily be the subject of an entire book in itself. For our purposes, we're going to stick to some simple solutions that help either hide or integrate the television with the surrounding art in a seamless manner.

The first solution is to do what comes naturally and accept that fact that you'll probably be arranging furniture such as couches and chairs around the television display. It's silly not to. Just as you might partition off a dining area with the use of art, keeping the functional aspect of a TV-viewing area separate from the rest of the living space can be accomplished in part with judicious art arrangements. This works only if you have the square footage and layout to accommodate such an arrangement—otherwise, you'll have to improvise.

From custom-built "easels" that can be rolled out when viewing, to makeshift curtained "theater displays" that hide the television when not in use, there are a variety of playful ways to approach either incorporating a TV into a room, or simply keeping it out of sight. But be wary of being too playful; a wall-mounted television can be interspersed among framed pieces of art as if it, too, were a painting, but that's a visual joke that might get old pretty fast.

Another way to think about the issue is to just consider the television another piece of furniture. We don't worry about a cabinet or a refrigerator competing with our wall displays—it's more about the emotional distance you might want to put between you and the device that you have to plan around. Setting a TV within a series of bookshelves or above a mantel can accomplish this—making it clear that it is indeed a piece of furniture. Excepting such overt solutions, a simple rule is to not put art any closer than eight inches from the edge of the screen—far enough to make it clear there's a different kind of object, but close enough that you're not making a statement.

DARKNESS AND LIGHT

What about the narrow hallway or the tiny apartment bedroom that faces an air shaft? Or the more innocuous north-facing room? There are plenty of decorating solutions for enlivening dark, smaller spaces, and marrying those techniques to the judicious placement of art can create a space that's both brighter and more emotionally alive.

Painting the space is the obvious first option. Tonally speaking, a bright, warm yellow can be more effective than a light, pristine white-painted wall in making a space feel larger. You can also accentuate the presence a window can have by framing it with open curtains. Art itself can play a factor as well, especially in helping set the perceived size of a room. If you hang artwork slightly lower in smaller rooms than you normally would, it can open up the walls above and create a larger sense of space.

Another, more dynamic solution is to play off the notion of opposite and contrast the smallness of the room with a large piece of art. This works best with more arresting and bold images, like oversize photograph blow-ups or big, ornately framed oil paintings that become the central visual focus of the space. Other, more decor-driven choices can also help, such as painting your floor white or keeping furniture minimal and chairs and tables open underneath.

When thinking about art as a part of your space, our end goal is to remove it from a secondary position. Hanging art is always the "last thing" people get to when moving into a new space; that's only natural, but it shouldn't be the last thing you think about when planning a space. Arming yourself with some basic planning tools like those in this and previous chapters can help you create living spaces that are artful and cohesive in ways that are much harder to achieve by accident.

The contrast between the deep colors of the walls, sharp sunlight, and well-placed art work to complete this space. *Stephen Kanner, Los Angeles, CA.*

An elegant kitchen corner, kitchen/entryway solution. *Cat and Dan Grishaver, Portland, OR.*

This nursery combines handmade mobiles with fabric art and framed prints. *Christine Schmidt and Evan Gross, San Francisco, CA.*

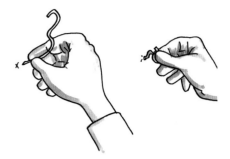
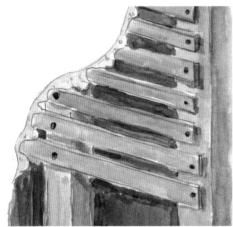

HOW

IN THE PRECEDING SECTION WE PLAYED GRAPHIC DESIGNER with the wall, arranging the best possible solutions for art from an endless variety of possibilities. Now it's time to play building contractor—we know where we will hang our art, now we need to ask how. The last section was all about theory and optics and aesthetics, now it's all about hammers and nails and anchors and plaster.

What's in a wall? Unless you happen to be a building contractor or you're intimately involved with a home renovation project, it's not a question to which most of us give much thought. But if you're going to affix something to a wall, it helps to know what exactly you're screwing or hammering into. If you approach affixing art to your wall haphazardly (as most of us do), it's not so much a question of you "ruining" your wall as it is of creating a lot more work for yourself, both in clean-up and repair, and in potentially hanging art that looks sloppy. If you do something haphazardly, it stands to reason that the final product will also look haphazard. And, of course, you can cause unsightly damage.

Whether you have brick walls or turn-of-the-last-century lath-and-plaster, you can hang almost anything with a little bit of foresight and the right tools. In the following chapters, we will discuss the basic of wall construction so you're equipped with the know-how of what you're hammering into, we'll detail the various tools and wall fixtures you'll need for art of all sizes and weights, and we'll chart out a few easy repairs for any mistakes.

But to return the question, what's in a wall? In most buildings, you're basically dealing with two kinds of structures, building walls and partition walls. Building walls, sometimes called load-bearing walls, are what support the roof—they keep the building up. Partition walls are the cosmetic walls that create the rooms we inhabit and help keep the heat in. In modern construction, most walls of both kinds tend to have a variety of components, such as a wooden two-by-four frame, insulating material, wiring and plumbing, and some sort of finishing surface, such as drywall or plaster, or brick. How you hang art will depend on both what the finishing surface is and what exists behind the surface. In the following chapters, we start with the most common types of wall and then detail a variety of other possible challenges you might encounter. For the most part, a trip to the hardware store for some very basic tools will be all you'll need. Just as in Where, we're going to show you the right way. That doesn't mean you can't get decent results by other, less considered methods, but doing so can be iffy. We know, we've done it. Sometimes you just have to hammer that nail into the wall and be done with it, planning and precautions be damned. It might work just fine, and if not, there's always plenty of spackle to be had at the hardware store.

HANGING ART
ON DRYWALL OR
LATH-AND-PLASTER
WALLS

Hanging art on your wall isn't rocket science, but it does help to know what kind of wall you're about to bore a hole into. Roughly 80 percent of the time if not more, the wall you encounter in your home will be constructed of drywall panels. This is a good-news, bad-news situation for the casual picture hanger. The good news is that for most of your everyday low-weight picture-hanging requirements, securing art directly into a drywall panel with a simple picture-hanging hook should do just fine. The bad news is that drywall doesn't take any sort of heavy abuse and hammering very well.

Sometimes called gypsum or plasterboard, drywall is a mixture of hard gypsum layered between two sheets of paper. Drywall replaced traditional lath-and-plaster walls as the standard construction material by the 1950s for obvious reasons—it's relatively cheap, carries less moisture than traditional plaster walls, and is easy to install. The downsides are that, being composed of paper and gypsum, it does not take water damage well, nor any kind of damage for that matter—it can be easily scuffed, chipped, or smashed. For most picture-hanging needs, however, unless your aim with a hammer is truly terrible, the most that you can do to drywall is put a few too many unsightly holes in it.

Previous to the ascendancy of drywall, lath-and-plaster walls were the go-to wall construction method. They are an ancient solution to the problem of just how to make a durable, heat-insulating, easy-to-paint-and-decorate wall. As with modern walls, lath-and-plaster walls start with a wooden framework, followed by laths: thin strips of wood that are secured in horizontal rows across the framework. The

What's in a Wall?

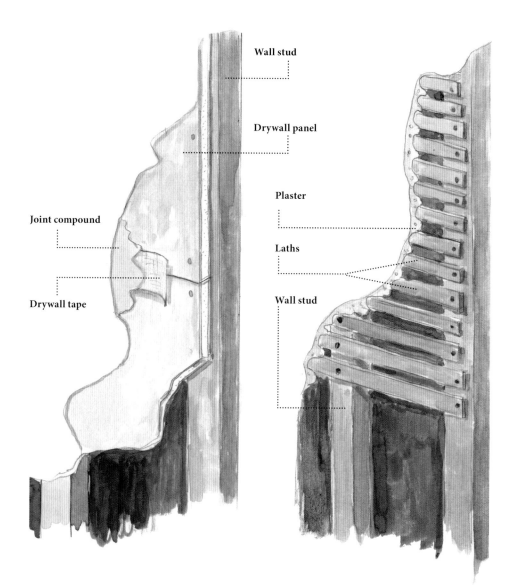

Wall stud

Drywall panel

Plaster

Joint compound

Laths

Drywall tape

Wall stud

DRYWALL CONSTRUCTION

**LATH-AND-PLASTER
CONSTRUCTION**

plaster is then applied in coats, drying between the laths, thus securing the entire wall surface in place. The application of and materials for lath-and-plaster walls changed over the ages, from plaster with a mud base to horsehair and other additives. The biggest worries from a picture hanger's perspective are crumbling the plaster when boring into the wall, or knocking the laths out of place and damaging the entire solidity of the surface wall.

LATH-AND-PLASTER OR DRYWALL?

Determining which kind of wall you have is an easy proposition. If you're a homeowner, you probably already know what your walls are constructed of, as you either bought it with drywall already in place, installed the drywall yourself or paid for its installation, or conversely had the antique lath-and-plaster left in place. As noted, drywall is common in almost all modern construction, but any structure built before the 1930s that hasn't been completely renovated may have antique plaster walls.

It's usually easy enough to tell just by looking and touching the wall. Drywall feels exactly like what it is, a smooth prefabricated material, while a plaster wall will have more of a homespun feel—more textured and harder. A crack in a sheet of drywall will feel chalky and sometimes you can even see the paper peeling from the crack, whereas a plaster hole will be more crumbled and malleable.

You can also check inside open seams, like say, an electrical switch box inset into the wall, or an unfinished closet or attic, to get a look behind the wall. Another test is to press a thumbtack into the wall. *(fig. 1)* Drywall panels are much softer than plaster—you should have no problem inserting a thumbtack into drywall, whereas plaster may give more resistance.

fig. 1

Keep in mind that in some homes, decorative coats of plaster have been added over drywall, either to create a more homespun look or to blend in with existing plaster construction and features in other parts of the interior. This shouldn't really affect any picture-hanging concerns as long as you know what's behind the plaster.

HANGING ON DRYWALL PANELS

People often ask "How much weight can drywall hold?" but that's unfortunately the wrong question to ask, or at least the answer you'll receive most likely won't reflect the reality of what you're trying to do. If you type that question into the search bar of your Internet browser, or ask somebody at a cocktail party, you'll get vague responses that seem to say drywall can hold about 20 pounds of weight from a single point. But if you asked anyone who works with drywall professionally the same question, they'd never answer with a distinct figure. Drywall can vary in thickness and strength, and how secure your art is on the wall will depend less on the drywall and more on what method you use to affix it.

Remember that drywall is basically a pliable substance of paper and plaster that gets its strength from being a cohesive unit; once you put a hole in the paper coating, the integrity of the panel is compromised. That doesn't mean a hole will make it fall down or fall apart, however. The big concern with art hung on drywall is that most often, you're hanging it from a single hook or fastener. Drywall can hold quite a bit of weight without any serious anchoring, as long as it's spread out and evenly distributed, but you put a lot more stress on a wall with a single point. And while the chance of seriously damaging your wall is slim, consider this: if it's easy to push a thumbtack into a panel of drywall, it's just as easy for something to fall out. Thankfully, there are a variety of wall anchors and fasteners that are easy to use and effectively anchor in place the weight of a framed piece of art.

WALL FASTENERS

Any well-stocked hardware store should have a variety of fasteners for sale, from basic picture-hanging hooks to more heavy-duty wall anchors. Just in case the staff at your local hardware store isn't as informed and friendly as ours is, here's an overview of the wall-fastening playing field.

Picture-frame hangers and hooks

These are your basic hooks, readily available at hardware stores and art supply shops under a variety of brand names (we've often bought OOK brand hangers), that use small nails driven into the surface of your wall at an angle. Simple to use and cheap, they are great for most lightweight pictures (say a framed eight-by-ten photo or print).

When using a simple picture hanger, nail into the wall at an angle with the tip of your nail facing downward at about 20 degrees. The same advice applies should you decide to not use a picture hanger at all, but just a nail (strictly speaking, such a method is not really advisable, but everybody does it, including us). Driving the nail at an angle into the drywall panel will provide a little bit of support by anchoring it against the weight of the panel, although if the item is too heavy for the drywall, it will eventually pull itself out of the wall.

"Professional-grade" picture-frame hangers

A step up in design and price, these hangers, by such brands as Hillman and OOK among many others, feature multiple entries for nails, as well as special "needlepoint" nails that are advertised as creating less damage to a wall. The nails also feature collars at their heads for easy removal. Some brands will give a weight capacity on

Wall Fasteners

PICTURE-FRAME HANGERS	Use to hang most lightweight picture frames up to several pounds in weight. Use multiple hangers to fasten heavier frames.	
"PROFESSIONAL-GRADE" PICTURE-FRAME HANGERS	Available in a wide range of styles, these hangers can hold heavier and larger-sized frames in place.	
"PUSH-IN" WIRE HOOKS	Not to be used with heavy objects, these hooks can be pushed directly into drywall for lightweight frames and objects.	
PLASTIC EXPANSION ANCHORS	For use with mid-weight to heavy objects, frames, and fixtures, the different styles of plastic expansion anchors all require a pre-drilled pilot hole for use.	
THREADED DRYWALL ANCHORS AND TOGGLES	Able to carry slightly more weight than plastic anchors, these fasteners offer more permanent solutions to fastening to drywall.	
MOLLY BOLTS	Another more permanent solution for heavy objects and large fixtures with multiple fastening points.	

the hanger's packaging, sometimes promising that the hanger can hold 100 pounds safely, but that seems a little excessive. Also, we tend to shy away from thinking of art by weight. How many of you know how heavy your framed art actually is? Who goes around weighing their art before they hang it? We suggest being careful—if your art seems big and heavy, then it probably should be hung with something more than a simple picture hook.

The whole idea with these tiny systems is that they help remove the play in the nail in the wall—if the nail is secure, the weight should be secure. We've successfully used these hangers to secure large framed prints to a drywall panel and encountered no problems. Their greatest asset is, by having more than one nail fastener, they distribute the weight more evenly.

As with basic picture-hanging hooks, affixing them to the wall is self-explanatory; mark off the appropriate spot on the wall and gently hammer the nails into place.

"Push-in" wire hooks

Several different companies make versions of these "no-nail-needed" drywall hooks. The curved wires are pushed into the drywall by hand (with a little shimmying and shoving on your part) until only the hook remains visible on the wall. The rest of the metal has pushed through the drywall and is wedged up against the back of the panel (kind of like when somebody in an old movie tries to secure a door by wedging a chair up against it). The hooks are cheap and easy to use, but no cheaper or easier than a standard picture hook, so choosing to use these hooks is really a matter of personal preference.

Mark off the spot on the wall where you wish to hang your hook. Measure up from the spot approximately quarter of an inch—this is where you will push the wire into the wall. Gently shimmy the wire into place. You can hang your art directly from the hook. *(fig. 2)*

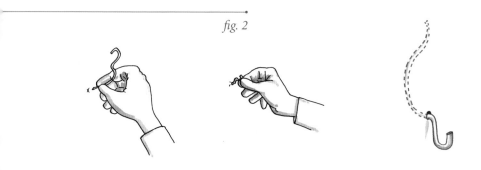

fig. 2

HOLLOW-WALL ANCHORS

"Hollow wall" means that you are not attempting to secure the fastener to a wall stud (more on wall studs below); instead you are sending an anchor through the wall's surface and into the hollow space behind it. The anchors have various ways of securing themselves to the back of the drywall panel. To be used effectively, most hollow-wall anchors require the use of a power drill. One of our favorites—with some caveats—is a no-nonsense version that uses a plastic sheath that, once inserted into the wall, expands outward and anchors against the back of the drywall panel.

Plastic expansion anchors

Mark off the spot where you wish to apply your anchor. Following the instructions that came with your plastic expansion anchor, drill an appropriately sized hole in the wall. Hammer the anchor into the wall.

Now, using a handheld screwdriver, install your screw into the anchor previously inserted into the wall, leaving enough room between the screw and the wall to hang your picture wire over it. *(fig. 3 - 6)*

Plastic expansion anchors are the least "strong" of the anchors available, but they're cheap and easy to use, and—given the physics of basic picture hanging—should work for *most* heavier but not *monstrously* heavy framed pieces. What we mean is that, generally speaking, a picture is hung on a hook, supported by a wire, so the weight of the object is

fig. 3

fig. 4

fig. 5

fig. 6

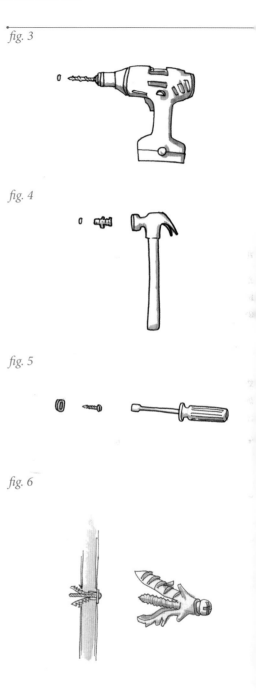

pressing downward against the wall. If you were hanging an object of the same weight that pushed outward, say a heavy-duty cabinet or sound system, the expansion anchor would be useless. For heavier picture frames, one solution is to use two expansion anchors to hang your wire from, spaced roughly an inch or two apart.

Threaded drywall anchors and threaded drywall toggles

These two options feature various improvements on the same idea as the plastic expansion anchor. The holding power of the threaded anchors is nominally more than that of the plastic anchors, and they tend to inflict more damage on the wall. Threaded toggles work on the same principle as expansion anchors, but then add a toggle that is inserted behind the drywall, expanding against the wall as you drive in your screw.

MOLLY BOLTS

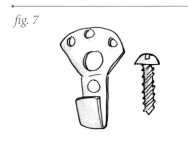

fig. 7

The molly bolt is one of the most secure wall fasteners available, but it poses certain drawbacks for the casual art hanger. It is basically permanent—the strength of the molly bolt comes from how it secures itself to the wall: it carves screw threads into the drywall, locking it into place. You can use a molly bolt on its own, leaving a little bit of a lip between the screw head and the wall to hang a picture wire on, or secure a picture hook with the molly bolt— you would, of course, need a hook specifically designed for use with larger screws. You can eyeball a proper hook by perusing the selection at your local hardware store and matching the hook to the size of your bolt, or you can buy specific picture-hanging hooks for use with larger screws. Hillman, for instance, makes a "masonry hook" that can do the trick nicely. *(fig. 7)*

To use a molly bolt, your process is very similar to all other expansion anchors, except that the molly is a self-contained device (rather than a sleeve that gets a screw inserted into it). First, drill an appropriately sized pilot hole in the wall per the instructions that came with your molly bolt. Next, tap the bolt into place until its head is flush with the wall. If you are using a heavy-duty "masonry hook" (as described above), place the hook in position over the bolt. Using a handheld screwdriver, turn the molly bolt clockwise. This activates the threads and secures the bolt to the wall. If you're not using a picture hook, you can leave a small lip between the screw head and the wall to hang your picture from. If you are using a hook, screw into place until the hook is tight against the wall.

WHAT ABOUT WALL STUDS?

"Just nail it to a wall stud" is the kind of advice you get a lot from folks who've never really nailed anything to a wall stud. It sounds like a good idea, but is it really sensible, practical, and easy? And is it any more useful than using the proper wall anchor or fastener? Studs are the framework of your wall; they're what the drywall sheets or lath-and-plaster are fastened to, the remaining space is filled with insulation, plumbing, and wiring. Obviously, hanging something from a stud is incalculably more secure than affixing it to drywall or plaster, but it is most often reserved for securing very heavy items, like a giant shelving or media unit, or extremely heavy pieces of art, lighting, or sculpture.

That said, if you want to hang art from a stud, go for it. Studs are easy enough to find, sort of. In most modern construction, studs are spaced sixteen inches apart. Begin by finding an electrical outlet on the wall near the location where you want to affix your object—outlets are generally affixed to studs—and then measure sixteen inches out from the outlet to find the next stud. Test your estimate by drilling into the wall: if you push through the plaster or drywall and hit wood, you've found your stud.

There are plenty of other ways to find wall studs. There are electric stud-finders that will make your job supremely easier and your pocketbook lighter (they range in price from ten to forty dollars or more). An unscientific technique is to drill a hole in the wall and use an unraveled wire hanger as a sort of divining rod. Create an L shape with the hanger, and while holding the short end of the L, insert it at a sharp angle so it's almost running flush along the inside of the wall. Push it along the wall's edge until you hit the wood of a wall stud. Measure off how far you inserted the hanger and an inch or so for the angle of the insertion and you should be able to find the stud (from there you can measure in succeeding sixteen-inch increments to find your next stud).

Remember that not all studs are made of wood. Aluminum wall frames are increasingly common in home construction, and are standard in industrial and commercial structures. To attach objects to metal studs, you'll need special tools and materials, including metal-drilling bits, toggle bolts, and mounting brackets. Because metal studs can vary, it's best to consult with professionals before beginning this process to determine exactly the right sort of drill bit and brackets needed for your particular wall stud.

WALL RAILS

Another option for heavy items is to take a cue from basic construction techniques and use a wall rail. Many elaborate hanging systems for shelves and/or heavy wall units work with rails. The rail is affixed to the wall, and then you affix your heavy item to the rail, thus distributing the weight more effectively.

This vintage nautical sign runs across multiple wall studs. *Chelsea and Noah DeLorme, Freeport, ME.*

Let's imagine you have a particularly heavy painting that you wish to hang on the wall. You considered hanging from a wall stud, but the ideal spot where you wish to hang doesn't have a stud behind it. What you can do is to create a rail that runs over the exact spot where you wish to hang your object, and then secure that rail to the two (or more) studs on either side of it.

First, determine the location of the wall studs to which you wish to secure your wall rail. Mark off the appropriate spots on the wall. Also determine where on the rail you'll be affixing your art. Mark accordingly.

Cut down a piece of wood for your wall rail. A one-by-two plank is generally sturdy enough to be of use. Obviously, you don't want the rail to be seen on the wall, so its length needs to be less than the width of the object you're hanging.

Using a power drill and the proper size of screw, secure the rail to the wall and into the wall studs. *(fig. 8)*

The best fasteners to use with a wooden wall rail will depend on what you're trying to hang, since how those fasteners will affix to the back of your art will vary. If you are hanging a heavy picture from wire attached to the back of the frame, your best choice would be to use special screws that feature a lip at their end that work as a hook. *(fig. 9 and 10)* The home brand Hangman sells these screws under the brand name Bear Claw Picture Hangers. *(fig. 11)* Affix two of these, spaced about an inch or so apart on your rail, to hang your wire from.

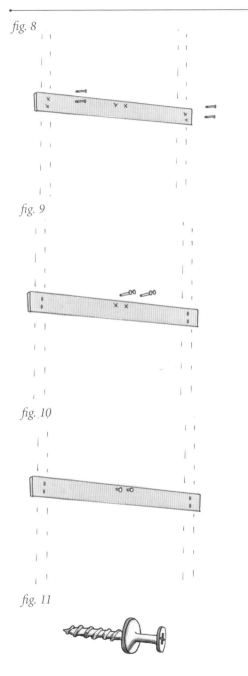

fig. 8

fig. 9

fig. 10

fig. 11

THE ELEGANT SOLUTION: THE FRENCH CLEAT

Even better than a wall rail is to use a French cleat. This is the go-to solution in many art galleries for hanging heavier framed art or art objects. It works on the same principle as a wall rail, but has an added elegance of design that ensures both an even distribution of weight and a level hanging. The cleat consists of two rails, cut at 45-degree angles on their top and bottom respectively. The rail with the cut on its top is attached to the wall, while the rail with the bottom cut is attached to the back of the art—the two pieces then simply slot together.

There are commercially produced French cleats available (they seem particularly popular for hanging wide-screen TVs and heavy-duty mirrors) that can be used for art as well. They are self-explanatory to install. Attach your wall rail to studs if possible. Make sure to use a level to ensure that the cleat is straight. Affix the other half of your cleat to the back of your art. There's no set rule as to where on the back of your art you should affix the cleat, but your best bet is to follow the same logic you would when hanging art from a hook and wire. The hook that your wire attaches to rarely rests at the very center or very top of your art, but usually falls somewhere about two-thirds of the way to the top of your art—so should your cleat. If your art is wider than it is tall, you can inch closer to the center of your art to balance the weight. As with hanging art from a hook, you'll have to measure ahead of time to ensure that your art is hung at the height you wish. If your picture frame is not constructed of wood, the French cleat becomes quite a bit more difficult to use, since you'll need to figure out a way to secure the cleat to the back of the art. Since French cleats are often used for heavier objects, they tend to be custom-built and -secured for the particular object.

How to make a French cleat for use with a wood picture frame

fig. 12

The benefit of making your own French cleat is that you can make it a custom size for your art, and it's fairly cheap: just the cost of lumber, a custom cut (if you don't have a table saw), and screws.

Measure out the desired width of your cleat. Purchase a piece of ¾-inch plywood at least twice that length. Cut into a strip approximately four to six inches wide.

Run this length through a table saw with the blade at 45 degrees, creating a beveled lip on one edge. *(fig. 12)*

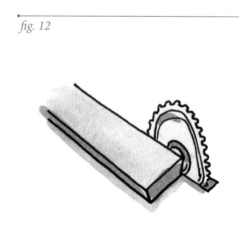

When not secured directly to wall studs, use hollow wall anchors to affix heavy decorative mirrors or other art objects to your wall.

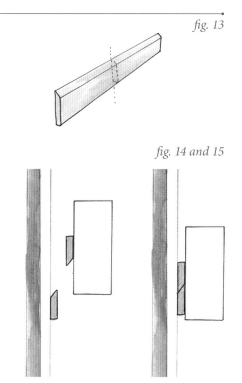

fig. 13

fig. 14 and 15

Cut the strip into two equal lengths—this will be both sides of your cleat. *(fig. 13)*

Affix half of the strip to your wall in the previously determined spot—ideally affixed to two wall studs. *(fig. 14)*

Secure the other strip to the back of your art, with the lip facing down and away. Use wood screws to affix the strip to the wood frame of your art.

Hang the art by slotting the two edges of the cleat together. *(fig. 15)*

The cleat, whether store-bought or homemade, is an elegant solution to heavy art, and probably the only one guaranteed to work that doesn't cause undue stress on your wall. The only issue for the casual hanger is affixing a cleat to the back of art that isn't in a wood frame. Doing so is not impossible, but requires a little care and planning.

OOPS! REPAIRING MINOR HOLES IN DRYWALL

If you're rearranging your wall hangings, it's probably inevitable that you'll need to patch your drywall a bit, especially if you're removing a wall anchor. Depending on the extent of the hole you're hoping to repair, your solution will vary. Most likely an unwanted hole made by hanging art will be no larger than a nail or screw and will require little effort to repair.

Patching small holes

You'll need a small can or tube of spackling compound. Spackling compound is your go-to product for small holes and minor wall-repair work—it's basically a gooey mix of gypsum and glue. Most any brand of compound available at a respectable hardware store will do the trick—for small jobs, you'll want to stay away from drywall joint compound, which is harder to work with (joint compounds, which are used for more extensive drywall jobs, are often powders that need to be mixed with water to use, although there are plenty of ready-to-go joint compounds available as well).

Take a small dab of the compound and put it on the tip of your index finger. Squeeze the compound into the hole you wish to fill, and smooth with a putty knife if necessary. *(fig. 16)* When painting over small holes filled with spackling compound, you shouldn't have to worry about having to prime the space to apply paint over it as you might with a larger repair.

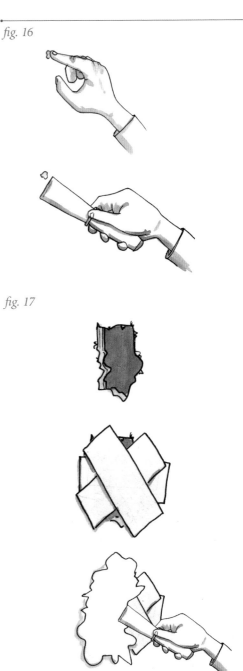

fig. 16

fig. 17

Patching medium holes

For larger holes in drywall (it can happen, especially if you're removing anchors or large bolts from the wall), say about the size of a fist or a baseball, there is a fairly quick fix that can be easily accomplished with a little compound and drywall tape.

Lightly sand the inner edges of the hole so you are working on a smooth surface. Lay strips of the drywall tape in a criss-cross star pattern over the hole, extending about three-quarters of an inch around the hole. Using your putty knife, cover the area (including the tape that has extended onto the wall) with drywall joint compound. In a pinch, you can use duct tape in place of drywall tape. *(fig. 17)*

Patching large holes

If you have a hole larger than three or so inches across, you might want to take a good long look at your wall-care activities and see what you're doing wrong. However, these too can be fixed. Here's a solution for a hole of about six or seven inches in width.

Lightly sand the inner edges of the hole so you are working on a smooth surface. Cut down a discarded chunk of dry-

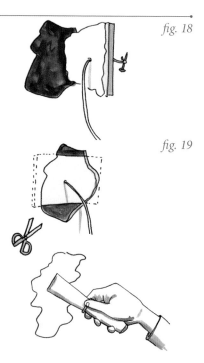

fig. 18

fig. 19

wall so that it's a few inches wider than the hole and yet narrow enough to slide through it.

Bore a small hole into the piece of drywall scrap. Slide a string through the hole and then tie a nail to one end of the string. The string will act as your "handle" to pull the drywall patch into place, so the side with the nail will be the back of the patch, facing the interior of the wall. Coat the sides and front face of the scrap with compound, and slide it (with the nail facing the back of the wall) into and behind the hole. (*fig. 18*)

Pull the string taut so that the drywall scrap is tight against the wall. Wait for the compound to dry the patch into place. Once it's secure, cut the string and fill the remaining cavity with joint compound. (*fig. 19*)

PLASTER WALLS

Hanging art from plaster walls is no more difficult than hanging from drywall panels, but if you're like us, the fear of causing permanent damage to your wall is amplified. Driving a nail into plaster just seems scarier than into drywall, maybe only because you know that your lath-and-plaster is probably decades old and hand-made. Or is it the resistance you're met with when you try to gently tap a nail into it? Maybe it's that chalky crumble that appears around even the smallest puncture in the plaster? As you stare up at the wall with your picture hook in one hand and your nail in the other, are you prepared to potentially ruin a fifty-year-old piece of artisan craftsmanship?

Despite those worries, affixing lightweight pieces of art to a plaster wall shouldn't be a stressful endeavor. Because lath-and-plaster walls are not mass-produced items, there's no way to state definitively how much weight they can hold or what sort of anchor would be "too big" to use on a wall.

Without affixing to a wall stud, we've hung large-format framed pictures (say about 20 pounds or so) on lath-and-plaster walls using a simple three-pronged picture hanger, and we've heard of people hanging heavier objects, but our feeling is that 20 pounds or so (in a picture frame, where the center of gravity of the frame and the hanger works to hold it in place on the wall) seems like the limit, at least philosophically. Heavier than that, or bulkier, you really need to consider other hanging options.

The big problem with using some of the hollow-wall anchors described above for the use of drywall isn't that they won't work—they can and have for many people—but they can also cause damage to your wall in a way that they can't in a drywall panel.

If you think about what a lath-and-plaster wall is, you start to understand the dilemma. If you're a inserting any sort of large bolt or anchor into the wall, there's a high possibility of it smashing into the lath. This might not be a problem; you might drill through the lath and have an incredibly secure hold—or you might hit the edge of the lath and crack or dislodge it. This, too, might not be a problem—plaster can be as hard as concrete and take a little abuse—or it might be ready to crack and crumble.

If you're planning on using anything more than various picture-frame hangers, proceed with caution. And if you're a renter and have a persnickety landlord, exploring alternative methods of hanging art might also be worth considering.

The contractors and professionals we spoke with recommended molly bolts as the best bet for anchoring heavy objects to a lath-and-plaster wall. Follow the instructions as detailed in the previous section.

Another option is to create a picture rail as detailed in the previous section, and secure it to two or more wall studs. If the object you're affixing is wide enough, you can also use this approach to affix French cleats to the wall.

Keep in mind, however, that for most picture-hanging needs, your basic picture hangers should do the trick. Plaster is tough—just be careful. Measure out where you want your art ahead of time so you're not sending a multitude of nails into the wall. If you're worried, it's always a good idea to use more than one to help spread the weight—space the two hangers between one and two inches apart, and adjust the picture-hanging wire accordingly.

Finally, there are plenty of ways to showcase art on plaster walls without using picture hangers or heavy anchors—we'll detail some of those (for use on plaster walls or otherwise) in later chapters.

A brick wall and colorful artwork in tandem for a pleasing composition. *Sasha Ritter and Kristin Morrison, Brooklyn, NY.*

BRICK, CONCRETE, AND CINDER BLOCK

It happens. You might end up living in a home with a picturesque brick wall running along an entire side. Or you might have a decidedly less picturesque cinder block or concrete wall that needs something pretty to distract you from its cold exterior. Or maybe you want to soup up your basement or garage work area with a little high art.

Whatever the case, affixing art to "solid" walls is actually quite easy, as long as you own (or can borrow) the right tools. And, there's no two ways about it, like Michelangelo chipping into stone to sculpt David, once you make a hole in your brick or concrete wall, it's there to stay, so measure it twice, three times, or four, and make sure you really want that art exactly where you drill—and that there isn't some alternative showcasing method to achieve a similar effect.

Each kind of solid wall has slightly different considerations, so we'll run through a variety of solutions.

BRICK WALLS

One low-impact solution for hanging on brick walls is to use picture-hanging clips designed for them. Available at most hardware stores under a variety of brand names (the Brick Clip being the most common), these clips attach to the bottom and top of a single brick, with metal teeth along the edge to grip the brick. The clips work

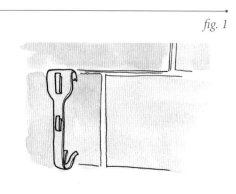

fig. 1

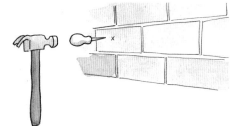

fig. 2

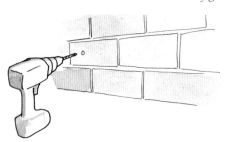

fig. 3

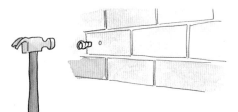

fig. 4

best when there's enough of a lip around the edge of the brick for the teeth to gain purchase—if the mortar is flush with the edge (or almost flush) you will need to reconsider, or try to chisel away at the excess mortar, which might be more of a chore. (*fig. 1*)

How much weight can a Brick Clip hold? The manufacturer claims a clip will hold up to 25 pounds when the object is attached to the clip with a picture wire, and online reviewers of the clips tend to have positive experiences, but the cynic's approach is to remember that results will be mixed depending on the center of gravity of what you're hanging and how firmly the clip is secured to the brick. If you're hanging something fragile or delicate (or heavy), it's probably best to consider another, more permanent method.

Another, more secure option is to use a lead expansion anchor, and fasten a masonry picture hanger into the anchor, or leave a small space between the lip of the screw and the wall to hang a wire from. Sometimes called lead screw anchors, these work on the same principle as the plastic and drywall anchors detailed in the previous chapter—as you screw the fastener into the threads of the anchor, it expands and locks the anchor into place in the wall.

Mark off the space on your wall where you plan to place the anchor. There's a lot of misinformation out there about whether you should drill into the masonry around the brick or into the brick itself. If you're using the anchor to hang a fairly large-framed picture, drilling into the

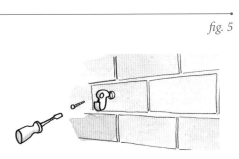

fig. 5

masonry should be fine, but you will have a more secure hold if you drill into the center of a brick. Obviously, use common sense: if the ideal spot for your anchor is near the edge of the brick, move it up into the mortar or down into the center of the brick accordingly.

You will need a power drill with a masonry bit. The instructions that came with your lead expansion anchor will tell you what size drill bit to use (the hole should be just a bit smaller than the anchor).

Use an awl to tap a small pilot hole into the brick (this will help guide the drill in and prevent wobbling). *(fig. 2)* Drill your hole. *(fig. 3)*

Use a hammer to gently tap the anchor into place until it is flush with the wall. *(fig. 4)*

Take your masonry picture hanger and place it over the anchor hole. Using a handheld screwdriver, insert the screw and fasten the hanger to the wall. *(fig. 5)*

CONCRETE AND CINDER BLOCK

You'll run into cinder block or concrete-block walls in more utilitarian construction, housing additions, and modern home construction. As with brick, attaching anchors to concrete or cinder block requires the right tools, and is a more or less permanent solution—while there are ways to cosmetically patch up holes in solid walls, drilling a hole into one shouldn't be done casually.

Although they get a bad rap as the de rigueur construction choice for bland college dormitories, what we commonly call cinder blocks have a lot to offer as a construction material. They're affordable, and can withstand extreme weather, flooding, and fire. They can also be sleek and stylish—cinder blocks have been used to great effect in many stylish and sleek mid-century modern homes.

The makeup of the blocks in your home may not be the traditional cinder and ash that we think of when we think of cinder block. They might be made from concrete or concrete aggregate—but whatever the makeup, cinder blocks will require special anchors and materials. When drilling into cinder blocks, depending on their construction or quality, you can create cracks or soft, loose, brittle holes—you most likely won't hurt the structural integrity of your wall, but a cracked and ever-widening hole around your fastener defeats the purpose of an anchor. Your best bet would be to practice drilling into concrete before you attempt the hole in your wall. Considering

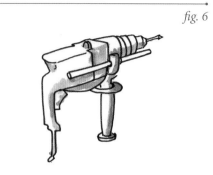

fig. 6

how cheap cinder blocks are, it's not hard to buy a few and give a quick whirl with the drill to see how it handles.

To make a hole in cinder or concrete block, you'll need a hammer drill, which is a power drill with a hammer-action setting—sort of a mini, precise jackhammer.

Hammer drill with the appropriately sized masonry bit for your fastener or hanger. *(fig. 6)*

You have two options for hangers, concrete screws or expansion anchors. As we've seen with other types of walls, expansion anchors provide more holding power. If you're hanging low-to-moderate-weight framed pictures, well-secured concrete screws should do the trick—but then, drilling into concrete is not the sort of endeavor you want to have to do twice, so why not use the anchor?

Either way, the first step is the same—you need to drill your pilot hole, into which you will insert your anchor or screw. An ideal placement would be into the solid section of the block rather than the hollow section, but an anchor can hold quite well in a hollow section.

From there, if you're using a concrete screw, you'll need to drive it into the wall with your drill. Slow, steady, and firm is the pace at which to proceed. You can snap screws, or tear the threads and diminish their holding power, so proceed carefully and confidently. If your screw still seems loose in the wall, remove it and place an appropriately sized plastic sleeve in the hole. The sleeve will help the screw threads find traction.

One final option is to use hammer-in, or hammer-drive cement anchors. *(fig. 7)* These work on the same principle as screw-in expansion anchors—they feature a sleeve that is inserted into the pilot hole, but instead of the sleeve being a separate piece, the hammer-drive anchor is an all-in-one item with a "nail" head at its base. Once you've drilled an appropriately sized pilot hole, you insert the anchor into the wall, and hammer the "nail" into place—this action will anchor the device securely into the solid wall.

fig. 7

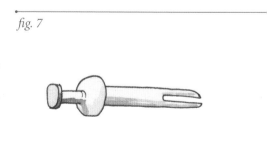

Since affixing objects to solid walls poses a number of problems, entrepreneurs and builders are constantly reworking and re-creating new anchors and fasteners. Do any of them work better than others? It's kind of like toothpaste—they're basically the same thing, and what you use is really based on preference and experience.

Especially if your art-hanging job is something more complex than trying to affix a few framed pictures to a solid wall, it's extremely helpful to consult with experts. Don't trust online forums that are full of half-baked advice—go speak to people who've had success with this sort of work, and proceed with care and caution.

A FEW SOLID-WALL TIPS NO MATTER WHAT FASTENER YOU CHOOSE TO USE:

1. Wear safety goggles when drilling into a wall.

2. After you've made your pilot hole, brush it out with a wire brush or vacuum it clean. The less chalk and dust in the hole, the easier it will be for your anchor to take hold.

3. If you require a pilot hole of a certain length, place a band of masking tape around your drill bit at the length you wish your hole to be, and then when the tape is flush with the surface you're drilling into, you'll know when to stop.

4. Be prepared for mistakes. What we mean is you can basically hammer away into a panel of drywall or plaster wall and not really do any damage that a little spackle can't fix. Solid walls present a little more of a challenge—while nothing really terrible can happen (structurally speaking) by drilling a hole into a concrete wall, it does require practice and patience.

5. And remember, affixing your art to the wall isn't the only way to showcase it. In the coming chapters we'll detail a variety of ways to display art (on concrete walls or otherwise) that don't require nails, hooks, or fasteners.

Prewar picture-rail moldings. *Lena Corwin, Brooklyn, NY.*

PICTURE-RAIL
MOLDINGS

Before the era of drywall, and before hollow-wall anchors and power drills, affixing heavy art directly onto plaster walls really wasn't a sustainable option. Instead, one had picture-rail moldings—decorative wooden moldings that ran along the tops of walls from which one could hang art. If you live in a home or an apartment with "prewar moldings," and they're not lacquered in layers of plaster or joint compound from years of neglect, they're quite easy to hang art from.

The two best things about picture-rail moldings are first, no drilling or holes of any kind are necessary, and second, it's very easy to move pictures from one place to another and adjust their height to suit your needs. There are a variety of different ways to use picture-rail moldings; we'll detail our favorite, which provides a clean, contemporary look.

Basically, hanging art from picture rails is self-explanatory. Using the aesthetic guides from earlier chapters in this book, determine what height you'd like the art to hang at. Then you measure out the amount of wire you'll need, so that the art hangs accordingly. From there you have a few choices as to how to affix the picture-hanging wire to the back of your art.

TOOLS:
Measuring tape
Picture-hanging wire
S hooks

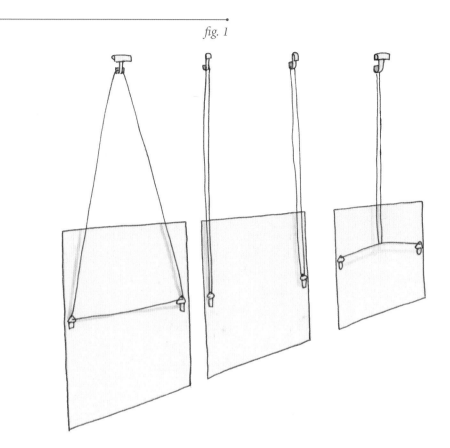

fig. 1

You can choose to hang your art from two S hooks and two separate wires. Hang each wire through the eye hook or D ring on the back of your art. If your art has no hardware, you'll need to affix simple screw-in eye hooks or D rings to it. Place your hooks anywhere between the halfway point of the length of your art and two-thirds from the top. The benefit of this hanging system is that you can easily measure out the exact length of your wire to ensure a level hanging, and more important, as when hanging directly onto the wall, distribute the weight between two points to ensure a more secure hold.

You can also string a single wire through each ring and loop it over the S hook hanging on the picture rail, creating a triangle shape with the loop of wire hanging from the hook.

Finally, if you'd prefer that only a single wire be seen running up your wall, there are two simple ways to do so. If your frame already has a picture wire running across its back, you can loop the wire through that and tie it to the S hook. Or you can add a single D ring—attached to the top center portion of your frame—and run your wire through that, tying it at both ends. *(fig. 1)*

TYING PICTURE WIRE

When hanging art with wire, you can use dedicated picture-wire hanging systems and cords, or you can use heavy-duty fishing line, which has the added benefit of receding a bit more into the background.

We can all make a knot with wire, the trick is keeping it taut as you try to secure it—especially important when you're trying to keep a wire the proper length so that your art hangs correctly. Here are two easy knots for various needs:

For attaching wire to D rings, loop the wire through the ring. Be sure to thread plenty of the wire through the ring before you begin your knot just to make gripping and knot-making easier. Fold the wire up and around itself. Then fold the wire back into the D rings, creating a slipknot. You can then take a bit of the excess wire and coil it around the tied-off section. *(fig. 2)*

The easiest way to create a taut loop for use when hanging art with a single wire is to create what fishermen call a "Surgeon's Knot." Loop both ends of your line through your D rings, and then, with plenty of extra line on each end, hold them parallel and pinch off where you wish to make your knot. Make a loose knot with both ends, and then lead your line through the open knot two times. Then, tighten the ends to complete the knot. *(fig. 3)*

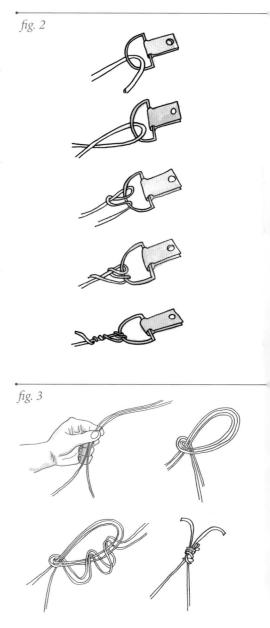

fig. 2

fig. 3

MOLDINGS

The devil in the details of prewar moldings is that, well, they're prewar. Especially in rental units, you might encounter molding that's been lacquered and plastered and painted over, or otherwise worn down over the decades, rendering it difficult to clip your hooks over it. Genuine DIY home-repair types would argue that the only true way to fix the molding in this scenario is to dislodge it from the wall and either replace it with new molding or chemically strip the molding and then put it back in place.

If you're a homeowner, replacing or repairing your molding makes perfect sense—from an investment perspective, you might even pay professionals to do it. If you're a renter, and are just looking for a quick fix so you can hang some pictures and not worry about them slipping and crashing down around you, rebuilding antique moldings might not be your cup of tea. You can ask your landlords if they'd be willing to repair them—you never know. Otherwise your best bet is to attempt to scrape and sand away enough paint so that your S hooks can get purchase on the lip.

Some home-repair suppliers sell special scrapers designed for the intricate grooves inherent in moldings, but since you're just trying to clear out the top of the lip, a simple putty knife should work to create enough space for your hook.

Picture rails don't have to be limited to use in prewar homes with moldings already built onto the wall. You can add your own moldings, or more modern-looking rail systems. The former is a fairly straightforward project that will require a visit to a home-improvement store. As for modern rail or "gallery systems," there are a variety of brand names available, which range in price and size. They work on the same principle as old-fashioned picture-rail moldings, but often feature a more sleek and modern look. AS Hanging Systems, for instance, offers stainless-steel rails with tensioned-cable hooks to hang art from, as well as more traditional approaches.

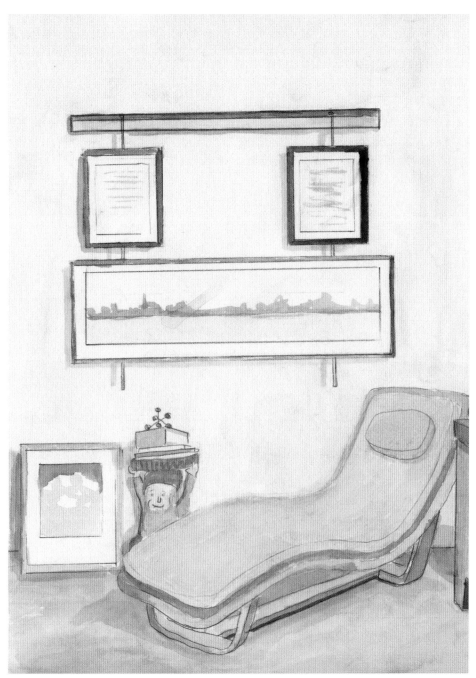

Easy-to-install picture rails are available in a variety of styles, both modern and vintage-inspired.
Anh-Minh Le, Portola Valley, CA.

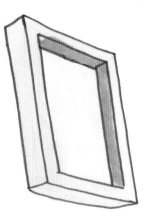

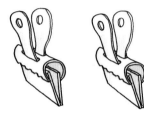

FRAMING

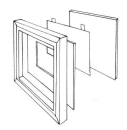

OUT OF ALL THE SUBJECTS IN THIS BOOK, framing is probably the one most destined to cause nail biting, indecision, and worry in the novice. How many people do you know with a blank wall in their new home and stacks of art "waiting to be framed," for months on end? And we all know why art framing lags on our to-do lists. You have to drag your art down to the framing shop, pay a lot of money, and then wait a week or so for the finished product. It's no wonder it's a task we tend to put aside, but if you want to graduate from thumbtacked dorm-room decor, it's inevitable you'll need to frame art yourself or get it framed.

We'd like to say that we're going to simplify the process for you and give you a low-cost DIY solution for all your framing needs, but the fact is there's a reason that professional framing is an expensive proposition. The tools and materials are expensive, cutting mats and building custom frames and mounting art all take time and expertise. Is the DIY solution—building your own frames and mats—any cheaper? The answer is it "depends," with a capital D.

If you were to purchase all the tools and materials you need to both build custom frames and cut custom mats, add in all the practice time and energy you'd need to expend to perfect your skills, you wouldn't be looking at a great return on your investment. Teach a man to fish, sure, but while fishing is something you might do every day to keep yourself well fed, framing is conceivably something you might do only in small bouts a few times a year. There are many fine resources for learning the A–Z of custom framing (we guide you to a few in the appendix of this book), but for casual users, we will take a page from Charles and Ray Eames, who aspired to make "the best for the most for the least." What's the most universally useful way to frame your art that is also affordable? The answer lies in some creative planning and purchasing.

Our approach works for a decent majority of framing needs: mixing premade frames with (potentially) custom-cut mats. In the coming pages, we'll walk you through the basics of how to plan the best solution for your art, be it a black-and-white photograph or an oversized oil painting on canvas. If you're starting from scratch and money is no object, you can follow the rules of visual aesthetics that we lay out in the pages to come, determine the right frame and mat for the work, and have it made by professionals.

If you're looking for solutions on the cheap, however, you'll want to use premade frames (or old thrift-store and yard-sale finds), and then you'll have to work out both the best-size frame for your art and mat—a math problem made easy with the charts and tables on the following pages. Add in a quick tutorial about how to mount art, helpful FAQs and a basic primer on the dos and don'ts of framing, and you'll have no excuse to not work through that stack of unframed art on your living room floor.

SIMPLE FRAMING SOLUTIONS
FOR WORKS ON PAPER

We'll begin with works on paper, as opposed to canvas or other more-textured materials such as needlework or tapestries. Works on paper mean literally that: a photograph, an original drawing or watercolor, an art print or lithograph, anything on paper. All works on paper are generally framed with a mat and placed under glass. The mat serves several purposes. It ensures that the art does not contact the glass of the frame, which would cause moisture buildup and inevitable warps and wrinkles in the art. It also acts as a visual anchor for the framed art, and finally, with a little planning, it's an easy way to fit an oddly shaped piece of art into a standard-sized premade picture frame (more on that below).

Anatomy of a Picture Frame

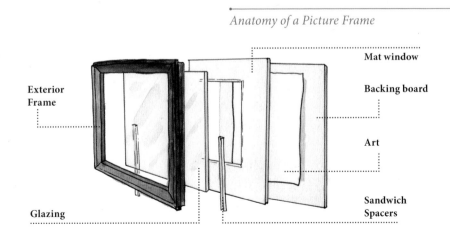

Exterior Frame

Glazing

Mat window

Backing board

Art

Sandwich Spacers

This mantelpiece features framed and matted prints. *Kate and Alden Woodrow, Berkeley, CA.*

Most standard works on paper are framed with the following components, working toward the back of the collection: The exterior frame, glazing (the glass), the mat, the artwork, and the backing board. Depending on your actual framing needs, there may also be some hidden sandwich spacers in the mix to further fill out the frame and keep your art free-floating.

However, first you need to decide how you want your art to interact with the frame and mat. This will partially depend on your personal taste, but also on the art itself. There are two basic routes to displaying art on paper in a frame: *bleeds* and *floats*. But that's kind of like saying there are two kinds of wine: red and white. Within those two options there are a multitude of ways to ably display art within a frame, protect it from decay, and preserve it for the future. We are going to stick to the basics—to give you a couple of good cabernets and a pinot grigio or two, so to speak, and provide you with directions, resources, and ideas should you wish to embellish further.

A bleed means that the mat opening or window "bleeds" onto your art, cropping it. A float means that the art hangs free of the mat window, leaving the edges of the art visible. Making the choice between the two options will have a lot to do with what sort of artwork you are framing and your own personal tastes—there's no set rule.

Basic Framing Options

BLEED   **FLOAT**   **MATTED FLOAT**

If the quality of the paper is an important aspect of the piece you are framing (say a gouache painting on a toothy deckle-edged paper), you may want to showcase it by floating it in the frame so that the object quality of the work can be easily viewed. Conversely, for a photograph, a simple half-inch bleed can be an elegant solution that focuses the viewer's attention on the image itself.

Your art, especially if it's a print or poster, may not "bleed" to the edge of the paper, but instead might have a space of blank paper around its edges. In framing parlance, this is called "carrier paper." In this case, you may choose to bleed the mat window into where the art actually "begins," or showcase a bit of the carrier paper, or float the entire piece. Basically, floating art treats the material more as an object or artifact, and bleeds lend the focus to the image as a stand-alone piece of art removed from the context of the material it is presented on.

THE SIMPLE, AFFORDABLE SOLUTION TO FRAMING ART

The easiest answer to the challenge of unframed works on paper is to determine the size of your ideal mat window and border and then attempt to find a preconstructed frame that can accommodate you. Never work backward and try to fit art into a particular frame size—always build outward from your art to determine the right components you require. After you've decided whether you wish to float or bleed your piece, you will need to measure your artwork to prepare for the next steps.

If you're planning on bleeding the mat into the artwork, you need to measure accordingly. Imagine you have a lithograph on 11-by-14-inch paper. The lithograph image itself doesn't bleed to the edge of the carrier paper, it instead starts about an inch in on all sides. You've decided that you want the mat window to bleed to the edge of the artwork, hiding the carrier paper completely. So your mat window should bleed over the paper an inch on each side, giving you a starting mat window of 9 by 12 inches. We say "starting" mat window as there's good reason to remain flexible about your mat window size.

If you're planning on floating that same lithograph rather than bleeding it, you'll have two options. You can float the artwork with no mat window (in which case the dimensions of the artwork will equal the frame window size, and which might require custom framing if the dimensions of your art aren't standard), or you can create a matted float, where your art rests free of the edges of the mat window. Let's say you've chosen this version, and you want your art to float behind a mat. You've decided you'd like about a half-inch border between your artwork and the mat window. So therefore your starting mat window would be 12 by 15 inches.

Once you've determined the size of your mat window, you need to figure out the best size of your mat border, and thus the frame you should use. While there's no solid rule for the size of your mat border, some of the same principles that applied when we discussed hanging art on the wall work here as well. You want your image to be optically centered, balanced out rather than overpowered by the frame and mat.

The chart below is used by many framers to come up with a basic guide for determining a workable mat border size. To use it, add up the length and width of your window size (remember, don't use the overall dimensions of the carrier paper—a common mistake!) and determine what is called the "united inches" of the piece. Then, look to see what you're starting border size is.

UNITED INCHES	STARTING MAT BORDER (INCHES)
9–12	1½
12–24	1¾
24–32	2
32–36	2¼
36–44	2½
44–50	2¾
50–54	3
54–60	3¼
60–64	3½

Now, the next step is to see if you can find a frame that fits the ideal size of your finished piece. Chances are you won't find an exact fit, but you can work out how to fit your piece into the closest available size.

We've listed a variety of standard sizes for preconstructed frames—these might not be available in every retail outlet or online shop, but it's a good guidepost to begin the hunt.

STANDARD PICTURE-FRAME SIZES (INCHES)		
5 x 7	12 x 16	24 x 30
8 x 10	16 x 20	24 x 36
8½ x 11	18 x 24	30 x 40
9 x 12	20 x 24	
11 x 14	22 x 28	

Let's imagine you have a silkscreen print that is 13 by 19 inches. The image itself is not full bleed, but has dimensions of about 10½ by 16 inches, with the artist's signature just below the bottom right-hand corner of the image. After some thought, you decide that you'd like to showcase a little bit of the "carrier paper" so that the artist's signature can be seen. You decide to bleed into the carrier paper an inch on each side, so that your mat window would be 11 by 17 inches.

Using the chart, you determine that your united inches (11+17) are 28, meaning that your starting mat border will be 2 inches. So, if you add 2 inches to each side of your mat window, you would end up with the outer dimensions of your piece being 13 by 19 inches.

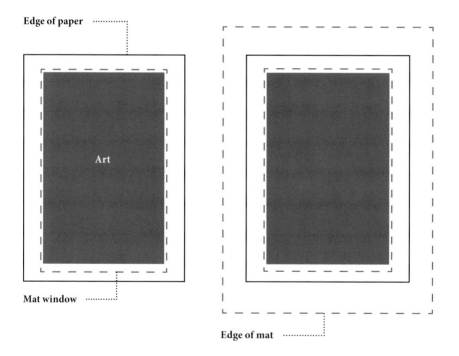

Looking at the list of preconstructed frames, your best bet is to use an 18-by-24-inch frame. This gives you mat borders of 3½ inches on each side, with 3 inches on top and 4 on bottom.

Now you need to buy your frame and get your mat custom cut. We'll start with the frame.

BUYING A FRAME

The whole reason you're using a premade frame and custom-cut mat is to save money, but we beg you, we urge you, don't skimp on the frame you buy! We've tested a variety of preconstructed picture frames, and like any other product, we've found that you get what you pay for. The big difference we found between cheaper frames and their costlier cousins is in the backing, and how the backing board is secured in place. On cheaper frames, the board may be a little wobbly or mis-sized, and more important, the fasteners you use to secure the backing into place will be shoddy and less secure. This causes headaches when you're securing your art in the frame, and afterward, your backing might bow out or be a little less taut than you'd like, making it more likely that your art will bow or wobble a bit. Basically, a shoddy frame can make your art look shoddy, or the very least, make your framing job more difficult.

We found this is especially true when buying a larger-size frame, say anything above 9 by 12 inches. A small shoddily built frame is still shoddy, but there's less room for its imperfections to become troublesome with a larger frame.

A note on frame glass or "glazing": If you're buying a preconstructed frame, the glass may or may not be actual "glass," and depending on what you're framing, this may be all right. Acrylic glazing is obviously cheaper, lighter than glass, and will not shatter when shipped. The low-end standard acrylic glazings offer no UV protection for your work, which again might be just fine. Light can affect artwork, but it depends on the medium. A photograph or inkjet print probably doesn't need UV protection under normal household conditions, but if it's going to be exposed to a lot of direct sunlight, then you probably should invest in acrylic or glass with UV protection. However, we'd argue that if your artwork is cherished or beloved or valuable, then you probably shouldn't be hanging it in a place where it's going to be exposed to direct sunlight for long periods, regardless of the protection you put into its upkeep.

Buying a premade frame and using a custom-cut mat will be cheaper than a professional framing job, but you don't want your finished product to look cheaper. Ask your local art supply store or frame shop what their favorite preconstructed frames are. They will probably be more expensive than the cheap ones you were eyeing, but the little bit extra will be worth it, and you will still be saving money.

CUSTOM-CUT MATS

The first rule of getting a custom-cut mat is "bring your art with you!" Even if you've gone through the above process and know the exact size of window you'll need, it's helpful to have somebody who does this job for a living take a look and make sure you're not overlooking something. Also, you'll want to match your art with the right color of mat.

Any retailer (either an art store or framing shop) that does custom framing should be able to cut a mat for you, but finding the retailer that's right for you and your needs will take a little trial and error. We've had great luck at our local art supply shop, where the framing specialists are able to both give us personal attention and turn around a custom-cut mat in the space of half an hour. But there can be framers who look at custom-cutting mats as busywork that gets in the way of their bottom line. Test the waters and shop around with caution.

What kind of mat? The days when you had to sincerely worry about the composition of your mat causing damage to your art are pretty much long gone. Once upon a time, mat board was made from the same sort of wood pulp that paper was made from. And with humidity and temperature changes, the acids that naturally occur in wood would eventually seep through the mat board and "burn" the art at the point of contact. With improving technologies, the days of inferior, art-damaging mat board are basically over, but the industry still plays off the fear of acid burn by providing the consumer with a variety of different mat board options that are acid free or acid-neutralized.

Today, most regular mat boards are acid-neutralized, and while they don't offer the same level of archival quality that cotton-core (which uses cotton instead of paper pulp) or museum-grade (also cotton, and lignin-free) mat boards do, they are not dangers to the preservation of your art. Then again, unless your output of framed work is so high that costs should be an issue, the museum-grade or cotton-core mat boards are not so much more expensive that it should be prohibitive to swallow the extra cost now and again for a little more archival safety.

What about color? Galleries and museums tend to frame art with a white mat—it's the good, solid default mat choice. It's classic and will always look good, letting you focus on the art and not on the mat. You can choose any color you like, but remember, styles and tastes will change, and a provocative color that catches your eye today might look garish in a year or two. White mats will never lose their timeless aesthetic appeal—they get the job done.

But even with white, you still have a multitude of choices. We speak more on color theory in other chapters in this book, but it's good to choose a tone of white that complements the art. If your art has a lot of royal blue in it, you want to pick a mat that complements those blues without overpowering them. There are cold whites, and warm whites and gray whites and brilliantly "white" whites. In the case of a deep blue, you can try to pick a white mat that has tones that are analogous with the blues in the work (that is, colors that neighbor the blue on the color wheel, blue-violet and blue-green) or you can choose a complimentary scheme (a color that is opposite blue on the color wheel, like orange). You are dealing with subtleties here—the whole point is to make the mat recede and the art pop. When working with the framing specialist who will cut your mat, you can put mat swatches against your art and eyeball them—some will clearly look better than others.

How much will it cost? Pricing will vary depending on the size of the art and the kind of mat you're purchasing, but our experience has been that buying a decent premade frame and getting a custom-cut mat should give you a savings of anywhere from 30 to 45 percent compared with a complete custom framing job. And speaking with the professional who will cut the mat for you is also a great primer on the skill and art of presentation.

For instance, let's return to our example. Let's say we've picked out our 18-by-24-inch frame and are now consulting with a professional framer who will be cutting the mat we've selected. We let the framer know that we need an 18-by-24-inch mat with a window that is 11 by 17 inches. If the framer is any good, he or she will look at your art and give an extra professional eye to the measurements you've provided, and perhaps make a suggestion or two. It could be as simple as discussing adding a weighted bottom to your mat (more on weighted bottoms later on in this chapter), or perhaps slightly reworking your window size.

Let's showcase one more example, this one a bit more problematic. Let's say you have a piece of art that is 7 by 9 inches, oriented in a landscape direction. This is fairly close to square, which will make finding a frame difficult. We begin by deciding that we will have a bleed of half an inch—meaning our window should be 6 by 8.

The united inches of 6 by 8 is 14; checking our chart reveals that our starting mat border size is 1¾ inches.

So, an ideal-sized frame would be 6 + 1¾ + 1¾, or 9½ inches, by 8 + 1¾ + 1¾, or 11½.

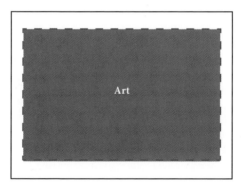

The closest standard-size frame is 9 by 12, which is just too small. You might be tempted to fudge on the mat border size and squeeze this art into the 9-by-12 frame, and if the art were vertically aligned rather than landscape, you could probably get away with it. But if you were to keep the window size of 6 by 8 and squeeze that into a 9-by-12 frame, you'd have 1½ inches on the top and bottom of the frame, and 1¾ inches on the sides. Strictly speaking, you don't want art where the side borders are wider than both the bottom and top borders. You can either equal them out or add extra weight to the bottom, but sides wider than the tops and bottoms creates a weird visual impression. You can do it, but it will look like a mistake.

At this point you'd have two options: you could bleed your window into the art a bit more, say a 1 inch bleed. This would give you a window size of 5 by 7. You could then fit this into a 9-by-12 frame with borders of 2½ inches on the side, 1½ inches on the top, 2½ inches on the bottom.

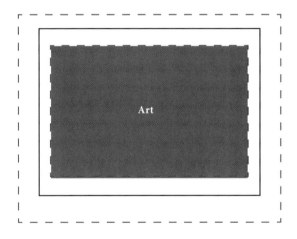

If your art can't take that closer bleed, you'll have to consider trying a larger frame. The next best standard-size frame is 16 by 20. That's a lot of space to fill with a mat, but it can be done. If you align the 20-inch side with the vertical side of your art, using the 6-by-8 window size, you'd have borders of 6 inches on the top, 8 inches on the bottom, and 4 inches on each side.

Another, more visually pleasing option would be to create a matted float using the 16-by-20-inch frame. Use a foam-core backing board and a mat that does not cover your artwork—your work would "float" on the foam-core back, and the mat would frame it within the frame. Your mat window size in this instance would be half an inch out from each side of the art, so 8 by 10 inches for a

7-by-9 piece (we discuss matting and floats and how to craft them with ease below). Using a 16-by-20 frame with the 20-inch side running vertically, you end up with mat borders of 3 inches on each side, 5 inches on the top, and 7 inches on the bottom.

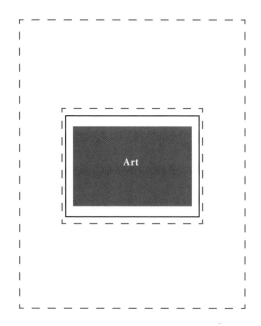

The only problem with this method is cost. You'd have to purchase a large frame, foam-core backing, and a custom-cut mat. It still will be cheaper than getting a custom framing job for your art, but you might be spending more than you'd like for a small piece of art, now in a rather large frame. It will look nice, but if you don't want to take up that much real estate on your wall, pricing out a custom-framing job might be worth it.

If you're going to the trouble of getting a custom-cut mat, can you also order a custom-made frame and then finish the job yourself? You can, of course, but at that point, the difference between paying a professional and doing it yourself isn't that much, depending on your framer. The big cost is the frame rather than the labor. Most frame stores don't make their own frames by hand, but order from a distributor—that's where the big cost comes in. Outside of frame shops and art supply stores, you can contact wholesalers directly, either online or through various catalogs. But why would you, really? Don't you want to touch and feel the frame you plan to buy, hold it up to your art and make sure it looks good? We're not advocates of buying frames or mats sight unseen online without a recommendation from trusted sources, or unless we've seen the materials ourselves.

WHAT ABOUT WEIGHTED BOTTOMS?

You'll note in the examples above, on one the top and bottom mat borders were equal, and on one, the bottom was wider than the top. This is called a weighted bottom—a convention in picture framing that you can choose to follow or ignore. *(fig. 1)* We've asked a variety of professionals about weighted bottoms and we've received different answers. Some say that the weighted bottom speaks to a genuine aesthetic principle (much like the notion of optical centering we discussed earlier in this book) that will make your framed art look better by creating the visual equivalent of centering. Others say it's just a convention that has persisted from a bygone era, and still others say it's an easy way for professional framers to use precut frame sizes when working on custom orders. Our thoughts are that it's probably a little bit of all three.

In the Victorian era, pictures were hung both higher and slightly angled (off picture-rail moldings), so an extra bit of mat at the bottom of the frame helped balance out a sense of visual vertigo. And that style did persist beyond the fashion of the day. And it is true that many professional framers buy precut pieces to assemble your custom-framed art, and that they might fudge the ideal proportions a bit to make your art fit properly—but a weighted bottom does somehow add a sense of elegance to a framed piece of art. If you take a look at any art that you have in your home that was professionally framed, chances are it has a weighted bottom. If you wish to use a weighted bottom when getting a custom-cut mat, you can either measure it out exactly beforehand, or go to your framer with your ideal mat window size and discuss rejigging the window slightly to add a weighted bottom.

THE FRAME PRIMER

All of the preconstructed frames we recommend in our resources section at the back of the book, from retailers such as Crate and Barrel and Restoration Hardware, are sleek, modern frames without a lot of embellishment. We recommend these types of frames because they are affordable and versatile—adaptable to many styles of art and the decorating choices within a home. But that doesn't mean they're the only choices you can make. There is a distinct artistry behind choosing frames for the art and the space it will reside in; it is a tradition that goes back centuries, and while you may not be framing a Rembrandt to hang in the secluded drawing room of your estate, it still is helpful to think about the classical approach to framing art.

Putting a border around art is pretty much as old as art itself, but the framing tradition that most influences our current choices dates back to the European Middle Ages. The earliest wood-framed artworks were pieces commissioned by the Church that worked as decorative elements and altarpieces within the interior of a cathedral. In other words, they were not meant to be moved or reused for another purpose (in

fig. 1

fact, some of the earliest European frames were carved from the same block of wood that the art was painted on). These altarpiece frames mirrored the Gothic architecture of the cathedral itself. When the newfound wealth of the Renaissance allowed fine painting to leave the church and take up residence with moneyed patrons and taste making royalty, this tradition of architectural elements in framing remained, as did the notion of tying the frame to the overall scheme of the space.

In his book *On Decorating*, Mark Hampton notes how this classical approach often had the surprising result of reducing the impact of a painting. Writing about a life-size portrait by John Singer Sargent, he notes that its original setting was dominated by the complementary architecture of the room it had been designed for. The Sargent, rather than hanging on the wall, "becomes part of the wall." He notes how the Sargent, now in a more modern setting (and in the same frame, minus a pediment embellishment) suddenly became more powerful, its full character revealed as it contrasted with the space around it. This give-and-take relationship is the key to any frame choice. The modern solution, borrowed from art galleries, is to let the frame recede and the art take precedence, but since art in the home is also decoration, you have all the tools of a decorator, and centuries of frame design, to play with that equation as you wish. Here's a brief illustrated overview of some of the basic frame types available beyond the modern, unembellished frame.

American Frame

The classic frame for a salty nineteenth-century maritime painting, the fluted cove style features a curved and gilded interior with distinctive but not overbearing embellishments.

French Frame

These frames reached their apex of design innovation in the eighteenth century under Louis XVI. They tend to feature rococo flourishes and gold leaf (imitation or otherwise). These are the frames that were most often paired with nineteenth-century Impressionist paintings.

Italian Frame

Frames of the style developed in the Italian Renaissance tend to be overtly architectural. Pictured here is the sgraffitto style, featuring a leaf pattern scratched on a dark wood panel.

Dutch Frame

The tradition of Dutch frames grew up with golden age of Dutch painters. These wooden frames feature ebony finishes and intricate checker-work designs. While a Dutch frame would be perfect for that Vermeer original you have gathering dust in the storage shed, they also work great for any painting with a darker overall color scheme, especially portraits.

Spanish Frame

These are deeply influenced by Italian and Flemish designs, but have a character of their own, reflected in intricate scrollwork that makes them look the most medieval of all the basic frame styles.

Mixing and matching frame styles works especially well on salon-style walls.

Mounting drawings, prints, and watercolors can be a simple at-home process.

MOUNTING
TECHNIQUES
FOR WORKS ON PAPER

After the frame and the mat are ready, the next step is mounting your paper-based artwork to the mat, or to a foamboard backing. There are a multitude of ways to showcase art in a frame—some are makeshift solutions, some are permanent and pricey, some are simple and versatile. We're going to focus on the solutions that are simple and versatile. The mounting techniques below are consistent, easy, and best of all, *archival*—meaning that the artwork itself rests free in the frame allowing it to expand and contract according to temperature and humidity, and it can be safely removed and reframed. The approach is called hinge mounting, and here's how it's done.

HINGE MOUNTING THREE WAYS

The T Hinge

This simple hinge mount will do ably for any work on paper where the mat window bleeds over the edge of the artwork (as opposed to a float).

What you'll need: mounting tape. Don't use Scotch tape or masking tape or electrical tape, or spit, or really anything other than mounting tape. As with any activity that people get anxious about, there are a variety of different kinds of tape you can spend your money on. Are any of them better than others? Well, for the purposes of hinge mounting, you can use most standard mounting tapes, or any labeled "hinging tapes." All mounting tapes are acid-free so they won't burn your artwork, most are self-adhesive, some can be removed by lightly dabbing them with water, some are double-sided. For hinge mounting, you won't want to use double-sided tape. If your artwork is very delicate and lightweight, and you're worried about tape showing through or affecting the integrity of the paper, you can look for mounting tissue—a more lightweight solution to tape. Additionally, you can purchase archival-quality museum-style mounting kits and all sorts of high-quality add-ons and extras. The goal of all the available technologies is the same: to cause minimum damage to your artwork and to mount with the least amount of contact between the art and the mat or mounting board. For most purposes this can be ably accomplished with hinging or mounting tape and a little care and planning.

To begin: make sure your hands are clean and that you have a clean surface free of dust, lint, or stray hairs (you don't want to go through the trouble of mounting your art and then notice debris stuck between the mat and the glazing). It helps to have an extra pair of hands when you're mounting, especially during the first few steps.

Precut two pieces of mounting tape; the pieces should be a little more than 50 percent longer than your mat window bleeds onto your artwork (so if you have a ½-inch bleed, cut pieces of tape that are a little longer than an inch). Gently place the tape strips on the edge of your work surface within easy reach.

Lay your artwork face up on your work surface and place your mat over the artwork—arrange it as you wish it to appear in the frame. (*fig. 1*) If your artwork is fairly large, this can be tricky. Grip both the mat and the artwork tightly, and if you're working alone, turn it over so that it is facedown; if you have a friend with you, hold it up. (*fig. 2*) Your friend can then make sure that the artwork and mat are free of debris, and that it is still in the best position for mounting.

fig. 1 and 2

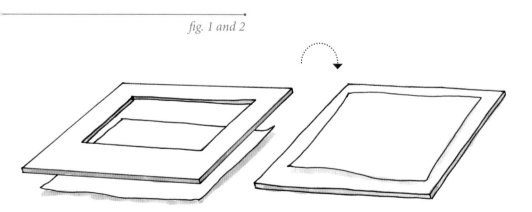

Now attach the two strips of tape to your art. Arrange them vertically, slightly in from the top corners of the art, say about half an inch to an inch from the edge of the art. Ideally, the portion of the tape that you've affixed to your art should equal the mat bleed onto your artwork. This helps ensure that a silhouette of the tape won't show through in strong light. So, if your bleed is ¾ inch and you are applying a 1½-inch strip of tape, half of your tape will be attached to the back of your artwork. (*fig. 3*)

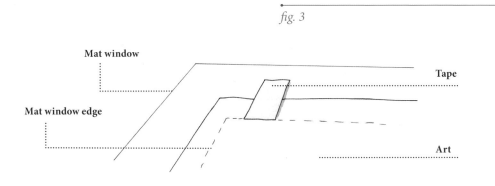

fig. 3

Mat window

Tape

Mat window edge

Art

Now you'll need to attach the other side of the tape strips to the back of your mat, creating the beginnings of your T hinge. (*fig. 4*) If your art is very wide, you may need to apply a third strip of tape between the other two hinges.

fig. 4

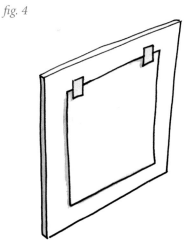

The tricky part at this step is making sure that your artwork is exactly as you'd like it to appear through the mat window—you want it hanging straight and unbowed. Once the tape is lightly affixed, turn the mat over and rearrange if necessary. Once the display looks good, you can more firmly apply the tape.

If you're working with a partner, one person can guide the artwork into place while the other tapes it from behind.

The final step of the T hinge helps create extra holding power without adding

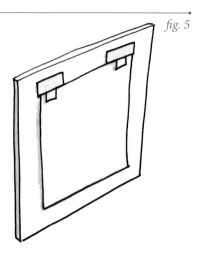

fig. 5

any more tape to your actual artwork. Apply two more strips of tape horizontally across the portion of the tape attached to your mat board. This creates the T in the hinge. These tape strips should only be affixed to the mat, and run flush with the top edge of your artwork. *(fig. 5)*

Your artwork now hangs free in the mat window and you are ready to place the backing board behind the art and close up the back of your frame. If you are concerned about your art being damaged by acids in the foamboard backing of the frame, consider lining the space between the backside of your art and the foamboard with a cotton-based sheet of lining or drawing paper—or any acid-free paper. There are special linen papers you can buy for this purpose, but any cotton-based paper will also work.

The S Hinge

If you are floating art in your frame, that is, if the mat board will not be touching the art (as described in the last chapter), you can't use the T hinge, since it would be impossible to hide the tape in the finished display. Your first impulse would probably be to affix a loop of tape to the back of your art, dorm-room-style, and plop it onto the backing board of your choice. You wouldn't be far from wrong— the preferred method, the S hinge, is basically a more elegant and more secure version of this.

What you'll want for the technique described below is mat board, cut to fit your frame. Mat board is acid-free, which is important for preserving the framed artwork, and it can have a subtlety of color that will be necessary if your framing plan calls for showcasing any of the backing (rather than having your art flush with the sides of the actual frame edge). Finally, mat board is easier to cut than foamboard (well, at least it's a *little* easier)—you will need to make incisions in the board to prepare it for mounting.

As we discussed earlier, there are numerous ways to float your art: You can choose to create a simple float, which is just the artwork floated on the backing board and placed in the frame, or a matted float, which features the artwork floated on the backing board with a mat window on top of it. The technique described next works for both.

First, position your artwork face up on the mounting board exactly as you want it to be displayed. If the edges of your art will not be flush with the sides of your frame, you'll need to mark off this placement in some way—very light hash marks just under the lip of your art might do the trick, or careful measurements with a ruler marked down on scrap paper (we prefer to measure exactly where the top corners of our art will be as an easy guide (two inches down, one inch in, for example). If you are creating a matted float, this would be a good time to also make sure your placement of the mat window is correct.

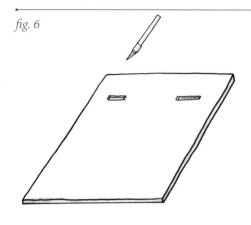

fig. 6

Remove your art (and the mat window, if using one) and, using a sharp mat knife, cut two horizontal slits (or narrow rectangles) in the mounting board. The slits should be about 1 to 1½ inches long and around a quarter of an inch wide. They should be placed about an inch or so in and inch or so down from the top corners of where you want your art to hang on the board. *(fig. 6)*

MAT KNIFE TIPS

Cutting slits into a mounting board is an easy sentence for us to write, but it's not necessarily all that simple to actually do.

Use a ruler to add hash marks for where you'd like your slit to start and end—especially useful because when you're using your mat knife to cut you might not see exactly where you need to begin and end your incision.

Don't force your cut, lightly score it. Using a ruler and your hash marks as guides, cut the long horizontal incision first, and then the tiny vertical cut, and then the bottom horizontal, and then the final side of the narrow rectangle. Work lightly, you'll need to pass over the cuts several times to ensure a smooth cut.

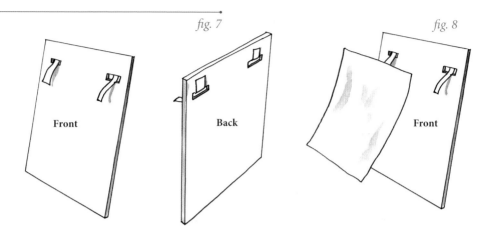

fig. 7   *fig. 8*

Front   Back   Front

Once your rectangles are complete, cut a four-inch piece of tape and feed it two-thirds of the way through the slit with the adhesive side facing the side to which you will affix the back of your artwork. Secure the portion of the tape you've fed through to the back by taping it down above the incision (creating a vaguely S-like shape for which this technique is named). Repeat for the other slit. *(fig. 7)*

You now have two strips of tape almost ready to secure to your artwork. For extra durability, you can then choose to secure the hanging tongues of tape to the front of the board with a tiny strip of tape, one for each tongue, applied in an upside down T shape at the bottom of the tongue.

Next, place your art gently onto the waiting tape. Once you're sure it looks straight and it is positioned correctly, press firmly. *(fig. 8)*

The V Hinge

Finally, there is one simpler, but less elegant, solution to mounting floats, the V hinge. This is an easier to accomplish, but it's also less durable and has the potential to look a little sloppy. We don't recommend it for larger artworks, but if you have, say, a small postcard-size watercolor or a 4-by-6 photograph, this can do the trick. The big issue with this technique is that if the artwork moves even a little bit, the tape hinge might be exposed to view.

Arrange your art on the mounting board as you'd prefer it to appear. Keeping the top edge of your art firmly in place, gently flip your art up and over, as if you're opening a trap door and the top of your art is the hinge.

Still keeping the top edge of your art firmly against the mounting board, place two vertical strips of 2½-inch tape that run half on the mat board and half on the back of the art. Now, create a T closure for each tape strip on the mounting board. The top of the T should run flush with the edge of your artwork. *(fig. 9)*

Now flip the art back over, and the art should hang with the tape hidden by the top edge of your artwork. You can see how the V hinge can be a little tricky—it requires careful placement, patience, and planning.

fig. 9

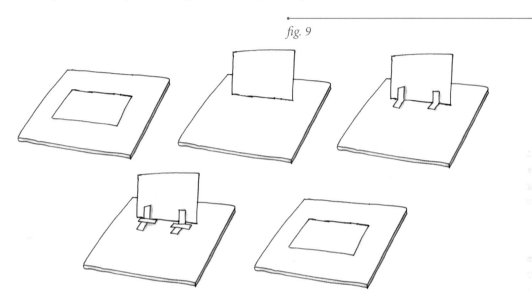

FINISHING THE JOB

Additional acid protection: While mat boards are acid free, wood isn't. So, if you're using a wooden frame, the acids in wood can potentially "burn" your art. If you're concerned about acid from the wood in your frame, picture-framing suppliers such as Lineco sell acid-blocking tape that you can use to line the interior edges of your frame.

How to clean your glazing: The big problem with cleaning glass that will be used for display in a picture frame isn't so much dirt as it is static electricity—which attracts dirt and lint and other minuscule debris that can make glazing look dirty. Additionally, if you're using a preconstructed frame, the glazing is most likely acrylic, which is even more prone to static buildup and scratches. Traditional household window cleaner is not your best bet for cleaning glazing (glass or acrylic); it can work, but it's prone to streaks and smudges that you don't see until after you've put your frame together and hung it on the wall.

Your first step is to be patient. Most of us tend to remember to clean the glazing just as we're about to complete the hanging of our framed art, but to properly clean glass and ensure it's free of lint and dust, you'll need to set aside a little bit of time before you begin mounting your artwork.

As noted, a household glass cleaner is not recommended, but can be used with caution and care in a pinch. Your best choice is a solution of warm water and white vinegar, or a solution of warm water and everyday dishwashing soap (the latter solution is the preferred choice for many professional window washers). For the vinegar solution, the ratio isn't that important—extra vinegar can't hurt or smudge the glazing—let's say two tablespoons of vinegar for every cup of water. For the soap solution, less soap is better, a healthy squeeze from the bottle for every cup of water—you want it mildly soapy.

Use cloth—ideally a soft flannel cloth. Lay your glazing out on newspaper. Dampen your cloth in the solution and apply it to one side, then wipe off the excess but do not dry it completely. Turn over and repeat. Now let both sides air dry. Air drying is the key to ensuring smudge-free glazing. If you attempt to dry the glass by hand with paper towels or a cloth, you'll only succeed in ruining the work you just did. You could be manically Type-A and wear cotton gloves while cleaning, or you could just be careful and hold the glazing with a cloth.

One final finishing touch to consider is adding a dust cover to the back of your frame. For the casual framer, this is almost purely a cosmetic addition. Professional framers apply covers to their finished works for a clean and seamless look; reports on the actual protective quality of the cover (basically a sheet of Kraft paper) vary. We recommend skipping this step when framing at home.

WHEN TO USE SANDWICH SPACERS

The goal of archival framing is to ensure that your artwork is protected from decay, usually from acids in wood-based paper and from mold and deterioration caused by humidity buildup. When you mount a piece of artwork behind an acid-free mat window, you're ensuring that the artwork has room to breathe; it's not pushed up against the glass, which can be extremely harmful to paper-based artwork. Condensation can build up on the glass and affect the work. If you are float mounting artwork and you're not using a mat window to buffer the artwork from the edge of the glass, you'll need to put sandwich spacers in the frame so that the artwork is not wedged up against the glass.

Sandwich spacers are easy to use, and also easy to make. They are long, narrow strips of acid-free material that are hidden under the lip of the frame, so the spacers will be in contact with the glazing rather than the art. You'll need to pick the spacer that fits for your frame and artwork. Consider them almost like shims for a table: you don't need to (but you can) line the entire frame lip with a spacer, but you do need to create an even surface for the art to rest against. Conversely, you can also make your own sandwich spacers by cutting strips of acid-free mat board.

When using an S hinge or a V hinge you will most likely require sandwich spacers, depending on the depth of your frame.

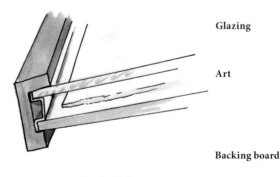

Frame

Glazing

Art

Backing board

Sandwich Spacer

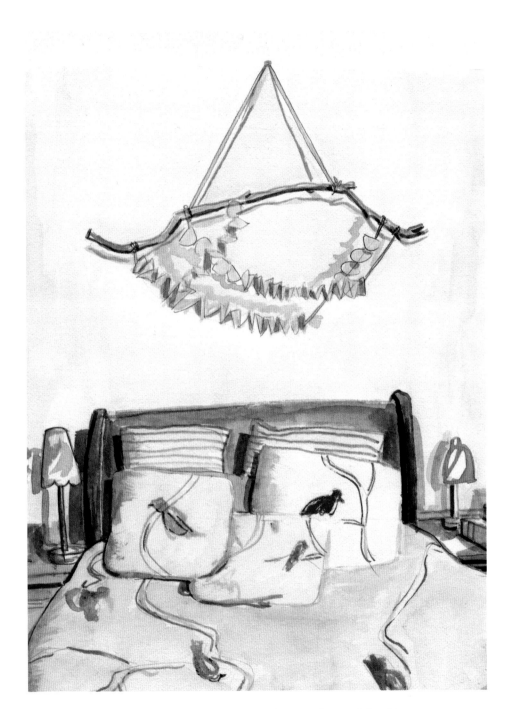

A simple branch sculpture hung with wire. *Kate and Alden Woodrow, Berkeley, CA.*

OILS, FABRICS, AND OBJECTS:
PRESENTATION AND FRAMING FOR CANVAS PAINTINGS AND BEYOND

No wall is complete without at least one work on canvas. Be it oil or acrylic, modern or classical, or a bizzaro thrift-store find, there's something about the boldness, color, and physical texture of a good painting on canvas that lends a sense of completeness to any wall. The same can be said for other non-paper-based pieces of art, from vintage tea towels and tapestries to historic memorabilia and mementos. This chapter will discuss some simple framing options, tips, and tricks for oil paintings and beyond.

PAINTINGS ON CANVAS

Any painting on canvas should not be placed behind glass. Canvas needs air, and glass obviously prohibits the breathing room that will help prevent rot in the material. Generally, canvas paintings are presented with no glass and no mat—just the stretched-canvas art lowered into a frame and secured with clips and clamps to its back.

Of course, this makes the DIY-light solution we've laid out for works on paper a little harder to accomplish for canvas artwork. There's no room to fudge with a canvas painting—if your painting does not fit the dimensions of a preconstructed frame, you'll need to go to a professional framer, or invest in the time and tools to build a custom frame yourself. And what makes it even harder when dealing with canvas paintings is that you not only have to worry about the length and width of your frame, but the depth—many conventional, store-bought frames that you'd use for a work on paper will not have the depth required for your canvas painting that is already mounted on wood stretcher bars (or a painting on a thick wood panel for that matter). You can indeed purchase premade frames built for paintings on canvas, but even then it's best to talk with a professional about the best way to achieve your vision for the artwork.

It's good to remember, however, that stylistically speaking, a painting may not need to be framed at all. It can stand alone on the wall—you can hang it from the wooden backing frame that it has been stretched on. Unlike with works on paper, there is no protective element to framing a painting on canvas—it's a choice of aesthetics. The only issue is making sure that the actual stretcher bars the canvas is attached to are strong and sturdy. If there isn't already a wire attached to the back of the stretcher bars, you can screw in two small D rings on the inside edge of the vertical stretcher bars, run picture wire through them, and you're ready to hang.

If fortune is in your favor, and the painting that you want framed is a standard size—or if it's not but you managed to find a preexisting frame that fits the art—and if the frame's depth works for your art (or is close enough that it won't look weird; more on that below), or if you had somebody build you a custom frame or you built one yourself or ordered one online (Whew! That's a lot of ifs!), here are your next steps.

If the art fits snugly into the frame, a professional framer would most likely use "points" to secure the art in place. Points are slim metal slabs that are similar to the tiny clasps often built into the backs of commercially constructed frames—except that these are more secure, since the framer drives them into the wood with a point driver, a device similar to staple gun. If you were to become a do-it-yourself custom-framing prodigy, a point driver would be one of the key tools (decent models cost about $80 to $100) in your household arsenal. *(fig. 1)* The points are affixed into the frame parallel to the back of the art, locking it into place. If you don't own or can't borrow a point driver for this operation, you can use brads—which are basically tiny nails that you tap in parallel to your art with a hammer. The problems with this method are obvious—you're swinging a hammer in a pretty delicate place, and probably not all that effectively, since you don't want to smack the frame itself out of shape.

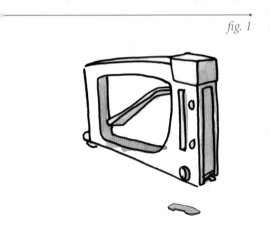

fig. 1

Your next option is a little easier and more versatile, if a little less elegant. This will also work if your painting doesn't quite fit into the frame (it's either too narrow or too wide for the frame). Offset clips are tiny brackets that come in a variety of sizes. One edge of the clip is pushed against the art, and the other is placed against the frame. You then screw the clip into the frame. Several of these placed around the art do the same job as points or brads. *(fig. 2)*

Both of these options, when completed at home with a found or preconstructed frame, are fairly makeshift. They'll get the job done, and if completed with care and patience, will look good, but this approach for paintings on canvas is stretching our "best for the most for the least" goal a bit. It would take a lot of luck for all the proverbial ducks to line up correctly—a decent frame, a borrowed point driver, a piece of art that fits the frame, and so on. Really, your best bet if you feel that the art needs a frame is to consult a professional. We've had great success at art stores, where you'll encounter students and artists who will approach your problem with a variety of solutions (as opposed to a frame shop where you might—and I say might—get up-sold a bit).

We talked with artists who frame their own paintings, and the general consensus is that if you're not building custom frames or getting a professional framing job, there's no other way but "makeshift" to get it done, since the needs of each particular piece of art will be unique. The Los Angeles–based artist Esao Andrews often buys frames online—his favorites are the Plein Air series from pictureframes.com, which, as Esao notes, have a "classic dark wood molding" aesthetic that complements the moody fantasias he paints. For his paintings on wood panels that are shallower than the depth of the frame, Esao uses a staple gun to drive staples partially into interior sides of the frame at right angles to the artwork—the staples act in the same way points or brads do to hold the panel in place. *(fig. 3)* Esao then covers the back of his frame with Kraft paper for a clean look, as we described in the previous chapter, although he uses rubber cement rather than white glue in a delicate process that he calls "an art in itself."

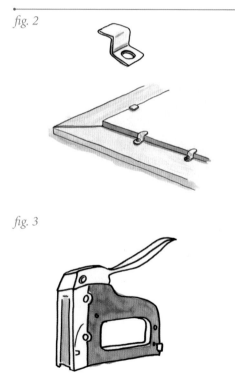

fig. 2

fig. 3

Shadow boxes can be homemade, store-bought, or makeshift.

When not painting on canvas, Andrews will use thick wood panels. To clasp these into the frames, he uses metal mirror holders, which work on the same principle as offset clips—S-shaped brackets that get affixed to the frame and hold the art in place.

Other artists we spoke with are fans of the staple-gun method, but tend to approach makeshift framing options on a case-by-case basis—and this is probably the best advice for you. Unlike with matted art where you can really make almost any art fit beautifully into a frame, art on canvas requires a little footwork. Thankfully, there are "standard" canvas sizes that artists can adhere to so that they can save money by stretching their canvas onto commercially produced stretchers rather than building custom stretchers. Frames for paintings are available in these standard canvas sizes.

What you'll have to determine is the cost for all this footwork compared with a professional framing job. Point drivers cost around $75, staple guns about $30, and points, brads, staples, Kraft paper, and offset clips can run your bill up a little bit more. And large frames suitable for framing stretched canvas, even when purchased preconstructed, can still run to a hundred dollars or more. Considering that a painting might be the capstone of your collection of art, it pays to give it your all on its presentation—whether that means a professional framing job or lots of makeshift care and extra planning is up to you.

DISPLAYING THREE-DIMENSIONAL OBJECTS IN FRAMES

A professional framer we spoke with noted that memorabilia framing is often the bread-and-butter foundation for a frame shop. That, perhaps, speaks more to the fact that fewer people frame art these days than they do memorabilia or mementos than to anything particularly expensive about the process. Our problem with a lot of framed three-dimensional objects is purely subjective—we think they can very often look a little corny and dated, or, especially if you're framing memorabilia, the wall of your home can end up looking like the display cases at a third-rate museum or Hard Rock Cafe. Our feeling is that less is more—the more simple and unobtrusive the display of three-dimensional objects, the better.

THE SHADOW BOX

When looking to display anything even slightly three-dimensional or objectlike, the wooden shadow box can be your best friend. It's not the only solution for showcasing objects, but it's a simple and cheap one. Wooden shadow boxes can be picked up art supply shops, or ordered online in a variety of sizes. One handy trick is to purchase premade wooden panels that artists normally use for painting (and which many art supply shops sell), and simply turn them around, creating an instant shadow box. Their depth makes them perfect for display, and the wood can be left unadorned, or finished and painted.

Our favorite shadow-box approach is to use the simple painter's panel flipped around, utilizing the lips of the panel as the sides of the shadow box. It's easy and fairly cheap.

Affix small D rings to the top corners on the sides of the box for easy hanging and then place your three-dimensional item(s) carefully on the bottom lip of the box. It might not work for every display need, but we like its simplicity and it beats having a bunch of knickknacks or mementos cluttering up the edges of shelves or tops of desks. You can also create a more curated display—dioramas or objects mounted on foamboard that is affixed to the inside of the shadow box. You can mount lightweight items by affixing fabric to the foamboard. Cut the foamboard about 25 percent shallower on all sides than the interior edge of the shadow box, wrap your piece of fabric around the board, and pin or staple the fabric (like velvet for a museum-style display) in place. Using "invisible" nylon thread (available at craft stores), you can sew lightweight items into place on the fabric, or purchase at craft stores more-elaborate systems for securing items (silicon glues and tiny clasps and clamps). When your foamboard display is ready, it can be gently placed inside the box and secured in place with pins. You can also buy preconstructed shadow boxes that feature glazing, especially important if you're displaying something that needs to be preserved (paper memorabilia, pinned insects, dried flowers, and so on).

FRAMING AND DISPLAYING FABRIC

The tactile quality and deep colors of cloth art, be it handmade needlework or a vintage quilt block, can add a certain homespun charm to a wall display. As with works on canvas, enthusiasts have developed a variety of makeshift techniques for displaying various fabric-based works in frames.

The two major issues with framing fabric are ensuring that the art is mounted in a manner that will allow it to be showcased properly and not wrinkle or crease, and preservation—ensuring that the work won't get worn by the elements. Mounting techniques vary, but as with works on paper, it's best not to use any technique that's permanent, so stay away from glues or other caustic adhesives, and get to know the power of pins and other simple tools.

SPECIAL CASE: BLOCKING AND FRAMING NEEDLEPOINT

Blocking is a term of art referring specifically to needlepoint canvas. A blocked piece of needlepoint means that it has been prepared on a board so that's its edges are aligned. Unblocked needlepoint can be loose and a little askew, with edges curling—basically not in the best shape for display. We recommend that, unless you're a needlepoint expert, it's best to get your piece of needlepoint blocked by a professional, especially since the joy of many needlepoint designs is in the exactitude of the stitched pattern. It's not a complex job, but it is time-consuming and requires lots of practice. Just so with mounting needlepoint for display—take it to professionals and let them get it at least as far as mounted on foamboard, ready to lower into a frame.

If you have a needlepoint canvas ready to frame, you can choose to use a mat window in its display or float it in a frame following the same principles detailed in earlier chapters for works on paper, with one major difference—you won't want to use glazing. You will see a lot of needlepoint framed behind glass, but technically, it shouldn't be. If you do choose to frame needlework behind glazing, you will want to make doubly sure (as with works on paper) that you use spacers (or a mat window) to keep distance between the fabric and the glass.

OTHER FABRICS

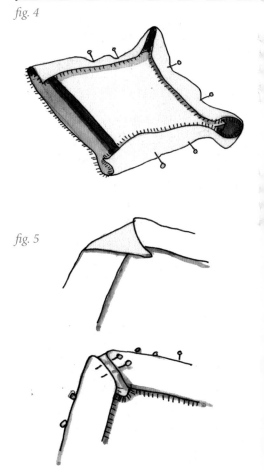

fig. 4

fig. 5

If you're not dealing with the special problem of needlepoint, you will still need to figure out a way to mount your fabric for framing. Since there are endless types of fabric-based art you might be framing (a vintage baseball pennant, a handmade tea towel, a colorful bit of patterned fabric), we can't supply all the solutions, but here are a few basic ideas.

Framing a tea towel (or other piece of stitched fabric). You will need foamboard, cut to the window size of your frame, tiny pins, painter's tape, and a ruler. Begin by ironing your fabric, then lay it on the foamboard face up. *(fig. 4)* If you're using a mat window, arrange the art in the window to your liking (since the edges of your fabric will be hidden by the mat, you can move your fabric as you wish to create a pleasing display). Remove the mat and place painter's tape on the edges of your fabric, lightly affixing it to the foamboard. Now take pins and slide them at a narrow angle through the edge of your fabric into the foamboard. Work from opposite sides. If you affix your first two pins near the top right corner, add the next two pins to the bottom left corner. *(fig. 5)* This will ensure evenly placed tension throughout so that the art will display without creases. One the pin work is complete, you can remove the tape. If you don't plan on reusing the fabric, you can cut away the excess bits with fabric scissors, or lay it flat. Place your mat over the art and lower it into your waiting frame.

If you plan to showcase the fabric without a mat, and you don't wish to use fabric adhesives, one option is to start by choosing a frame with a window smaller than the overall dimensions of your art. Cut your foamboard to the size of the window and arrange your fabric on the foamboard. Gently turn the foamboard and art upside down, and fold the edges of the fabric over the foamboard. Affix to the back of the foamboard with pins inserted into the board at sharp angles. Fold the corners snug to the back of the board, the closest you can get to "hospital corners," and pin them down. Add sandwich spacers to your frame and lower the mounted fabric.

The above method is akin to how artists stretch canvas onto a wooden frame in preparation for painting, and is adaptable to a wide array of fabrics and materials. We've heard of home framers using cardboard or a wood panel instead of foamboard, and staples instead of pins. The archival quality of these other methods might not be ideal, but it does get the job done. Speaking of which, should you have a sturdy piece of vintage fabric, one easy display method is to purchase a stretched, unpainted canvas on a wooden frame, and stretch the fabric over it. The frame should be

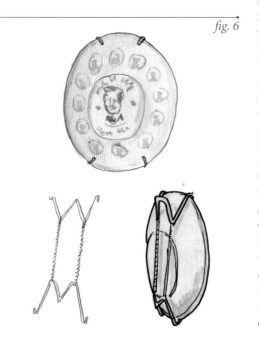

fig. 6

slightly smaller than the fabric, by at least four inches or so on each side. In this case, you will have to use staples to secure it to the back, and since the edges will be seen by viewers of the finished piece, you can't skimp on folding the corners back snugly and neatly. The best way to do this is to approximate "hospital corners." On one side of your fabric, staple all the way to the edge of the corner, but leave the other side slightly open. Now pull the side with the full line of staples toward you, gently but evenly so that it is taut. Now tuck the excess bit in gently, pushing the fold in as you pull it back toward the sides with the staples. The "fold" should be flush with the back edge and flush to the backside of the canvas. What this will do is stop a fold from being visible on the side of the stretched fabric. It's a minor issue, but it can make a difference. Now you continue stapling the remaining bit of fabric leading up to the fold, and repeat for all the corners, leaving you with a tautly stretched fabric over the canvas, and with the addition of D rings and picture wire to the back of the wooden framework, you have a ready-to-hang instant piece of art.

PLATES

Plates are easy to hang and can work as decorative accents on a wall or as compositions in their own right. You don't have to present the full Mrs. Grundy treatment and hang Victorian embellished floral plates in the kitchen. The colorful commemorative plate or treasured family heirloom can be used to add some texture and shine to an art display, or you can create a wall of plates on a theme or showcase a collection. Plate hangers—the basically spring-loaded clasps that attach to the back of the plate and are then hung with a nail or a screw affixed to the wall—are simple to use. *(fig. 6)*

THE OVERSIZED POSTER

Sometimes a traditional frame just won't do, but you still want to set the art apart and showcase its unique nature. One distinctive option, especially useful for large posters, prints, or ephemera, is to craft a wooden hanging system for the piece. For instance, we found a vintage educational poster at a flea market, and it sat rolled up for many months—it was a good find, a cheeky and colorful curio, but quite large (about 30 by 40 inches), and it seemed a little fussy to spend a lot of money on a large frame and a mat for a novelty that we might tire of over time. We did want to display it, however, and dorm-room-style thumbtacks just wasn't an option.

Recalling the manner in which maps and charts were once displayed in schools, on pull-down rollers, we decided to create a cheap-and-easy hanging system for the art, using wood laths and heavy-duty art clips. *(fig. 7)* This is a perfect way to display large-format posters or prints. We wouldn't recommend it for an item you wish to display for long periods of time (years and years, we mean), or something that needs special care or preservation— it's a loose and simple method.

fig. 7

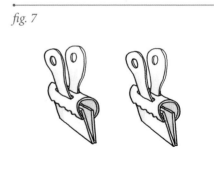

Start by acquiring four lengths of wood laths (say about ¼-inch thick and 2 inches wide), cut slightly longer than the width of your art. You can choose to paint the wood beforehand, or leave it unfinished for a more homespun look.

Lay your art face up on your work surface and place the wood on the top and bottom edges of your art, one underneath, one on top. For a good grip, you will have to have the wood flush with the edge of your art, so you will lose about two inches of visibility on each end of the art. The taped sides of the wood should be against the art, to help secure the paper from any potential acid burn.

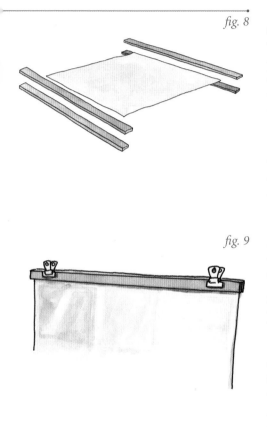

fig. 8

fig. 9

Once the art is in place, attach the two clips to the top pieces of wood, each about two to three inches in from the side edge of the art. Repeat on the bottom. The heavy-duty aluminum art clips have quite a bite, and depending on how heavy your art is, may be all you will need to hold the art in place. (*fig. 8*)

Now mark on the wall where you'd like to hang the art—this is easy if you know the width of your art and the exact location of your two hanging clips. For hangers, your best bet is to use a plastic drywall anchor, and then affix the screw to the anchor, leaving enough of it exposed so that the clip's top hole can slip over the screw. Once the hangers are in the wall, you can gently lift your art and place it on the wall. It should hang straight, about an inch or two from the wall. (*fig. 9*)

If the work is too heavy to be held by the clips, you can secure the ends of the wood (remember they were cut to be longer than the width of the art) more firmly with tiny nails, or wood glue. Or you can add more clips at the top.

An oversized educational poster hung with wood and wire. *Beth Salvini, Brooklyn, NY.*

OTHER ESSENTIALS

THERE ARE MANY PATHS TO ACHIEVE THE SIMPLE PLEASURES that come from possessing a wall of art displayed with creativity and charm. As we've seen, there's no shortage of "rules" you can follow, and rules you can break; there are various manageable skillsets to learn, master, and then ignore if you like. The enjoyment of art is such a subjective experience that it's hard to cement down a single way that art should be hung. One of the great things about working on this book was speaking to a variety of designers, artists, curators, and other creative people about how they approached hanging art in their own home. It was not so much the vast number of different approaches (and there were indeed many) but the fact that people would often come to the same solutions but for different reasons. Take the case of using shelves as a method to display art. For some people it was purely a space requirement—a small apartment or cluttered space—while others approached it as a way to break up their displays, creating a flow from one wall to another. Still others used shelves as a place to display rotating collections of art and curios.

In the next two chapters, we approach two sometimes overlooked, vastly different essentials in the world of hanging pictures: shelving and lighting. Like so many other aspects of this book, the skills we'll discuss are a mixed bag of design principles and simple home-improvement know-how.

Shelves and bookcases can do double duty for art placement.

SHELF LIFE:
OR,
HOW NOT TO HANG
A PICTURE

A shelf is shorthand for civilization. There's something about getting your mess up off the floor that's philosophically satisfying in a way that few other simple activities can be—just think about your last move, when you finally broke down that last box of goods and put away its stuff. It's the same thing. Shelves as a method of display share so much with art hung on walls—yes, a shelf is a piece of furniture, but unlike a couch or a footstool or a bed, we really only interact with a shelf on a visual level. We don't sit on them or eat on them or cook on them—we basically just look at them. A successful shelf stores items in a way that makes it easy for us to retrieve them when needed, and in a manner that is visually pleasing—just by virtue of the real estate a shelf can take up, it needs to look good. A shelf, basically, is a piece of functional art.

Now that we've got that semantic leap out of the way, let's get into the sandbox and start playing.

PICTURE LEDGES

Whether handmade or store-bought, picture ledges are an ideal way to create rotating displays of art. Lifestyle and home goods stores sell premade ledges in various lengths, widths, and materials. You can also build your own on the cheap, although you will need some special tools to make them in a manner that's both sturdy and visually satisfying.

Framed art and collections and picture ledges. *Lisa Wong Jackson and Nick Jackson, Berkeley, CA.*

POCKET-HOLE BUILT PICTURE LEDGES

A picture ledge can be any level surface attached to your wall, so they're fairly easy to improvise. You can stain and finish a two-by-four, cut it to a desired length, and attach it to your wall with a series of metal L brackets. Or you can use a wall shelf as a dedicated picture ledge, but if you're looking for a sleeker and less jury-rigged ledge, you'll need to do a little woodworking. The problem with hanging a flat surface on your wall is how to affix it. Store-bought ledges usually provide self-contained hanging brackets that are either hidden or are a seamless part of the design. Restoration Hardware, for instance, sells wooden wall ledges that come with metal hanging brackets that complete the found-object quality of the finished ledge, while other commercial versions feature hanging systems completely hidden by the inside lip of the ledge to create a seamless design.

One way to create such a ledge on your own is to create a sort of U-shaped ledge that has a shallow lip in front and a more substantial base in the back (that will then be bolted to the wall). If you've done any sort of woodworking, however, you know that crafting solid corners that hold together securely is a challenge. In the past such constructions would have been built with a slot-and-tab system and plenty of wood glue. Nowadays, you can easily create what are called pocket holes with a simple tool system. Pocket holes are shallow, angled holes for screws that are created by using a pocket-hole joinery system (sold most commonly under the brand name Kreg Jig). The system allows the user to create angled holes for screws so you can join two pieces of wood together securely. Pocket holes provide a tight and secure joint for wood, and they can be hidden inside the apex of the joint (rather than on the outside edges of a work), creating a clean finish.

Pocket-hole built picture ledge

Backing board

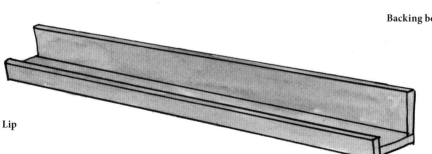

Lip

Base board

Along with the Kreg Jig you'll also need sawhorses and a few clamps—so this is indeed a genuine woodworking project, and not to be undertaken casually. As you'll see below, the jig works as a guide to allow smooth angled insertions into wood (the depth of your hole is easily set with a scale on the side of the jig), and it uses self-tapping screws—that is, screws that create their own pilot hole in the wood for a more secure hold.

Here's how to build two four-feet-long pocket-hole picture ledges, but you can cut them to whatever length fits your needs.

> 1x4 board, 8 feet long
> 1x3 board, 8 feet long
> 1x2 board, 8 feet long
> power drill
> Kreg Jig kit
> self-tapping screws
> sandpaper
> hollow-wall anchors
> workbench with clamps

The final ledge will feature a baseboard (the one-by-four), a backing piece (the one-by-three), and the smaller front lip (the one-by-two), which together create the U shape of the ledge.

Cut each wood board in half, so you have two sets of four-foot lengths. Set aside one length of each pair: you'll use that to create your second ledge (you can also choose not to cut the wood and create one long, eight-foot ledge).

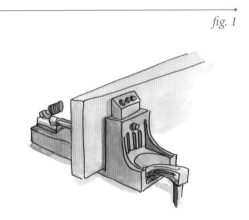

fig. 1

Lay your baseboard down on your workbench, and measure out spots for your pocket holes. You'll need holes to attach both the front lip and the backing (although since the screws are self-tapping, you need to drill pilot holes only into the baseboard). Space your holes anywhere from twelve to sixteen inches apart.

Follow the instructions with your pocket-hole jig kit to affix it to your workbench, and set the depth for your pocket hole—this is fairly self-explanatory: the kit will show you where to align your drill according to the depth of your wood. Be sure that you actually do measure the depth of your wood, however (board sold as being one inch thick is usually about three-quarters of an inch thick, since the wood is planed before you purchase it, losing about a quarter of an inch).

Clamp your wood into place and drill your pocket holes at the places you've marked, one corresponding to the backing and one for the lip at each measured space. *(fig. 1)*

Next you'll need to drill the holes for the anchors that will suspend your finished ledge on the wall. You'll be attaching these anchors through the backing board of the ledge directly into the wall. At this point, you're simply creating the pilot holes for the anchors. Space them about eight inches apart—follow the instructions that come with your anchor regarding pilot-hole size.

Clamp your ledge together, aligning everything up properly. Now you can screw everything together with a power drill.

Once the ledge is constructed, you can sand, finish, and paint it to your wishes. Then it's ready to be anchored to the wall. You can fill screw holes with wood putty and paint over them accordingly. *(fig. 2)*

Alternately, you can construct a version of this ledge without pocket joints, but it won't be as strong. You would need to use a combination of wood screws and wood glue (affixing the screws horizontally through the bottom of the backing board into the baseboard of the ledge, and repeating the process for the lip). Be sure to hold the constructed piece firmly together with clamps until the glue is dry.

However you make your dedicated picture ledges, how you showcase them on your wall is the fun part. You can opt for a conservative arrangement, one that works off the existing features of the room—a ledge above a sofa or a mantel (with the art arranged on the mantel as the first "ledge" in a series of two), for instance.

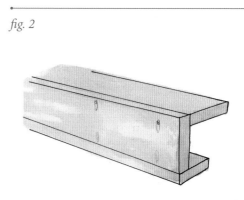

fig. 2

THE LONG LEDGE

You can also attempt displays that speak to the unique qualities of a picture ledge. There's something about that long, unbroken line that begs to remain "long." Imagine art shelves like wainscoting, running the length of a wall or perhaps wrapping around a room. Or a series of picture

Red and blue kitchen collection. *John and Linda Meyers, Portland, ME.*

ledges that run up from a kitchen counter, arranged with a mix of art, kitchen knick-knacks, and cookbooks displayed face out.

STACKED LEDGES

Another approach is to prepare a unique arrangement that fits particular pieces of art—making a sort of jigsaw puzzle that mixes traditionally hung art, shadow boxes, and differently sized ledges. Just as you would a salon-style wall (see the section The Salon), it helps to plan this out entirely beforehand on large sheets of paper so that you can create a powerful arrangement before you've put a piece on the wall. Use some of the same rules from a salon-style wall—try to use an anchor piece and build around it, and allow the three-dimensional nature of the ledges to work for you in creating depth and space.

One of the most compelling approaches to the picture ledge that we've seen involves layering artwork on long stretches of stacked ledges. With the ledges equally spaced in height from one another, you can use a mixed approach to display a large collection of art, both framed and unframed. As smaller images rest in front of larger ones, and small objects round out the array, it takes on a sort of collage-style pinboard feel.

COLLECTIONS

Since a shelf will often have another use rather than solely displaying art, it's important to be considerate about what you choose to showcase. A personally curated collection, whether it's beloved ephemera, natural objects, or more straightforward "art," will always be interesting to you (since you put it together!), but to make it visually appealing to others (rather than looking like just a bunch of stuff) can be tricky. For some tips, we turn to the San Francisco Bay Area artist Lisa Congdon, author of the book *A Collection a Day*, which chronicles a year she spent amassing 365 simple yet beautiful collections.

Congdon's advice: Keeping things off balance is key to an attractive collection. "Typically it's best to use an odd-numbered assortment. Odd numbers are easier to balance in general, and asymmetry is usually the most pleasing to the human eye." But of course, asymmetry alone isn't enough—just as we learned when arranging items on a wall, you need something to anchor the collection, either visually or thematically. "Arrange things that have some unifying factor," Congdon advises. "Like different bottles or vintage school supplies."

Color can also be a unifying theme for otherwise disparate objects, as can using the entirety of the space you've devoted to the display area. "Cluster objects fairly close together, and use the entire depth of the space," says Congdon. "To make arrangements appear balanced, arrange items of different heights together, placing the taller items toward the back and center of the cluster."

A desktop collection

Think about a collection as you might think about arranging a floral display, allowing highlights to pop out of the central theme, using size and repetition as much as variety of imagery to tell a story. Congdon's last bit of advice is to "step back" from the display to determine if you've achieved a balanced arrangement, and then reorder the items if necessary.

BOOKSHELVES

Short of building shelves and ledges dedicated to art displays, we often just want to use shelving fixtures we already have to do double duty. The goal in creating a mixed display is to make your intention—and the intention of the space—clear. In other words, if your bookcase is low-slung (say about hip level) and you want to avoid its natural tendency to become a table-like deposit area for loose change, keys, and remote controls, you need to create an art display that ensures you won't misuse the space and make clutter: consider bookending the display with large pieces, and evenly space items to craft a sense of authority.

If your bookcase is higher than table height, you can line the top with large paintings. The lower shelves can feature the occasional single art object or smaller collections. Don't line every shelf with art—try to create a sense of flow between the functionality and beauty of the books on the shelves with the display quality of the art. (We've seen some cool bookcase displays where books have been stacked atop one another with art placed atop them. While this looks really cool, as lovers of books, we sort of bristle against the notion of removing book browsing from the equation—books are meant to be picked up, after all.)

The sides of bookcases don't have to be fallow spaces—although they might be blocked off by walls or other furniture, when they're not, they can be used as spaces for display (you can use S hooks and picture wire as you might for a picture rail if you don't want to affix directly to the bookcase. We've also noted some bookcases where art is hung on the front façade, affixed either by picture wire or hooks directly over the shelves, or hung on hooks directly on the shelf. Like the stacked-book approach, we worry that while this can look striking, it diminishes the utility of the shelf, and therefore seems like a flawed approach. Another option is to make the content on your shelf part of the display—attractive coffee table books or LP covers facing out—and place small art objects in front of them.

Color-coded books and art displays on shelves. *Youngna Park and Jacob Krupnick, Brooklyn, NY.*

Sturdy benches, or low-slung bookcases can be used in tandem with picture ledges placed higher on the wall. *Carol LeFlufy, Los Angeles, CA. Inspired by a photograph by Marcia Prentice.*

WORKSPACE SHELVES

The functionality of shelves in a workspace—be it at home or in the office—is a given, but function can live hand-in-hand with the aesthetic diversion of art. The important aspect with workspace displays is to ensure that they don't impede the actual work that needs to get done in the space. Keeping objects off the desk is one way to draw the philosophical line in the sand, another is to turn efficiency into a display itself. Objects and art can be used as bookends for artfully displayed volumes, while files and other supplies can partner with visually compelling work to create a space that is both easy to utilize and comfortably alive with creative energy.

BENCHES

The bench begs to be used as an item of utility—but low-slung benches (or makeshift benches of stacked boxes, stools, and crates) can act as a sort of way station for otherwise orphaned art, houseplants, and collections. Sometimes the simple act of getting art off the floor is all that it takes to make a statement—try using a large piece on a bench, surrounded by smaller items staggered at different heights.

When working with shelving, art begins to cross over into the realm of furniture, so your understanding of the space you're utilizing (and the space you're displacing) becomes of added importance. You art is leaping off the neutral space of the wall and entering a more three-dimensional sphere, so your best bet is to approach such an endeavor as sculpture—and the shelf the art sits on as more than a frame—so that it becomes part of the art.

Wall lamps work both to showcase art and aid nighttime reading.

LIGHTING

It's a rare home where lighting is specifically installed to adhere to the needs of the art on your walls. Just as we saw with shelving, lighting serves a multitude of purposes in a home, and for most of us, the more basic requirements of lighting outweigh any specific needs art might require from it.

But what are those specific needs, if any? Broadly speaking, art is meant to be viewed in natural light—that is to say, diffuse and steady, not bright and blinding or dim and murky. Thankfully, aside from specific areas like workspaces or kitchens, you probably want diffuse lighting in your home as well—light that invites people to linger and get comfortable. In short, the light in a room should not be something you notice overtly —if you're surprised at how dark or how light a particular room is, it's probably lit incorrectly (unless it's a dive bar or a biological laboratory).

The easiest way to accomplish lighting that is conducive to viewing art is to have multiple light sources for a space. This doesn't mean to light your home like you would a football stadium—you don't need every centimeter of space illuminated, but you do need layers of light to gently brighten the room. Existing overhead lighting is often ill-suited to this purpose, at least on its own. A mix of floor lamps and table lamps can add dimension to your lighting—remember that one of the joys of lighting a room is that you are free to explore outward and upward. At the very least, you'll want more than one source of light, ideally at different heights, but as we'll see below, the light sources aren't necessarily as important as how you use them.

CONTROLLING YOUR LIGHT SOURCES: DIRECTION, DEFLECTION, AND STRENGTH

The era of incandescent bulbs is over. Although it may not be *legally* over (at least in the United States), continuing to use them, in the face of new and more energy-efficient technologies, is at best short-sighted and at worst irresponsible. We won't get into the politics, but it's pretty clear that consuming large amounts of energy by using outmoded technologies is not the best way to use energy resources or your paycheck. The biggest argument against switching to new light-bulb technologies is obvious: it's easy to find soft, warm incandescent bulbs at what we've come to think of as reasonable prices. In relation to art, what you want is exactly what incandescent bulbs can easily deliver—warm "daylight" glow. The options are changing, however. The bulbs we tend to think of as energy-efficient are the compact fluorescent light bulbs, or CFLs (the coiled bulbs coated in white). They are long-lasting and save you big on your energy bill, but admittedly, give off a pretty harsh and unnatural light. Your best bet, should you wish to purge the incandescent bulbs, is to switch to LED (light-emitting diode) bulbs. They cost more than incandescent bulbs, but they will last a lot longer (industry estimates give a standard LED bulb a 50,000-hour life span, compared with 1,200 hours for an incandescent, so we're talking years as opposed to months). Consider the upgrade in cost like switching from a throwaway foam cup for your morning coffee to a reusable travel mug.

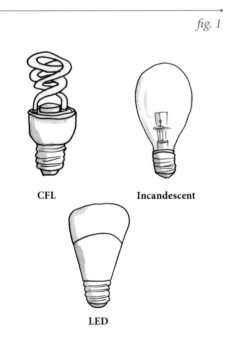

fig. 1

CFL   **Incandescent**

LED

And LED bulbs can easily supply the sort of light experience you will require. Various consumer research groups have run comparisons since the advent of LED bulbs, and all show that as the industry adapts, more and better LED bulbs are becoming available. Since the bulbs do cost more, you shouldn't buy any sight unseen. Visit lighting stores or the lighting section of your hardware store and find the bulb (and test it) that best suits your need. If you're replacing an incandescent, you'll most likely be looking for an A19-style bulb (A19 is the classic screw-in light bulb shape). Keep in mind that, as with any emerging technology, there's still a large discrepancy in quality—test and research before purchasing.

If you're dealing with a lamp, your next step after you've chosen your bulb is to determine the shade—which can have a huge

Multiple light sources help dispel shadows and create optimal viewing for art. *Jordan and Paul Ferney, San Francisco, CA.*

effect on the tone of a room's light. Remember, the rules of color we discussed earlier can apply even to something like a lamp shade. Colors have a deep effect on the light cast on artwork. As the Russian abstract artist Wassily Kandinsky noted in his typically dramatic fashion, yellow can produce a "painful shrillness," while red has an "unbounded warmth." He saw color as a balance between warmth and coldness, with warm colors moving toward the viewer and cold colors receding. When thinking about the interaction of your light source with both the wall and the art on it, the color wheel can still help you. At least in its relation to viewing art, the goal of lighting is to create a pleasant symmetry with its surroundings rather than a heavy contrast. The effects might be subtle, but the more you think about them, the more you notice them.

If your space features white, cream-colored walls, light or lamp shades that have a bluish cast to them can merge with the yellows of the cream to create a sort of greenish pallor, whereas a red shade (a bold choice no matter what, in relation to art) placed in a room of paneled wooden beams or walls can deepen and complement the chestnut tones of the wood.

Finally, as far as strength of the bulb is concerned, that remains a little to your personal taste—but do remember that powerfully bright light sources are not best for creating diffuse lighting.

PICTURE LIGHTS

Picture lights, like you see in museums or in the wood-paneled libraries of well-to-do estates, are a soft-focus way to get around the whole diffuse-lighting challenge. They work best with large-scale framed artworks, as they lend a sense of authority to the work, but it's a tactic that's hard to use sparingly—if you light one painting on a wall, it would be odd to not then light them all. (Another reason this tends to work best on a wall with large paintings: there are fewer objects to light.)

Store-bought options for traditional picture lights range from plug-in fixtures, which require wall outlets and a tolerance of unsightly wires, to battery-operated models. They are small, soft-focus lights that illuminate a work and draw the eye toward it, and their use is fairly self-explanatory.

Affixing "picture lights" to your wall crafts a very particular visual statement, one that might not match the mood you wish to create. Here are a few other ways to illuminate a room more thoroughly.

Consider wall mirrors as a way to indirectly amplify light sources in a room. You don't want to place the mirror directly next to the light source you're trying to amplify (you shouldn't be able to see the lamp in the mirror when looking at it head-on); instead, it should be placed on a wall that receives illumination both from a window and from the room's light sources.

Traditional picture lamps work with frame choice to create a complete composition.

The light-colored floors and the soft wood tones of the walls help create a lighting scheme that is conducive for art display. *Interior design by Tara Mangini and Percy Bright of Jersey Ice Cream Co.*

Remember that light sources placed at different heights and locations around a room are the key to diffuse and even lighting. When viewing art, you don't want all the light to come from one direction or a single powerful source, especially if that source is "behind" you as a viewer. This can be a challenge even in a room with ample natural light, if that light is coming from a single set of windows; consider a floor lamp on the wall opposite the main light source to balance out heavy shadows.

Light a shelf or a bookcase. This works particularly well if the shelf has a lip or edge. String soft white Christmas lights along the edge of the lip so that the bulbs are hidden from view—keep the string of lights taut and even, and hide the wires behind the bookcase. Alternatively, you can hide the lights behind the books or items on the shelf. If the Christmas-light solution is a little too dorm-room chic for you, there are integrated lighting systems available from lifestyle retailers such as IKEA that can create a more refined look and are easy to install. Another option that can work on its own or in tandem with shelf lights is to paint the interior of your bookcase a warm and bright color to help spread illumination and create a visual hit of color and brightness without being overwhelming.

There are more permanent and expensive solutions, like installing lighting in your walls or ceilings—anything from track lighting to sconces or wall lamps. However, you can also trick out the space's existing lighting features to make them more amenable to your tastes and better suited to illuminating art. Removing standard-issue overhead lighting fixtures and replacing them with more creative options can make a world of difference on many levels, from setting the tone of a room to more standard illumination issues. Depending on the room, don't be afraid to go big with chandeliers or pendant lights (they always seem bigger in a retail environment than they will in your home). Experiment with paper lanterns or work past the sticker shock and invest in a high-design lighting fixture—one quality piece can change a room entirely. Whatever you do with overhead lights, be sure to also install a dimmer switch—this will be integral to controlling the space.

Sometimes it's not so much that your lights aren't working as it is the environment that they are attempting to light. Repainting a wall in a warmer, brighter shade of white, for instance, can help illuminate a space. Or in mixed-use spaces like open kitchens, where there's lots of dark space underneath cabinets, consider tiling walls with clean, cool-white subway tiles that will help usher more light into the space.

DEALING WITH DAYLIGHT

Over time, direct sunlight can indeed harm your artwork, even if it is framed behind UV-protective glazing (also, remember that there is no such thing as non-UV light—every light source gives off ultraviolet rays). Oil paintings can darken or brighten when exposed to direct sunlight and should be showcased in dimmer environments (hence the use of picture lights in museum settings). Professionals recommend that oil paintings should be hung in spaces that have a luminance measurement of 200 lux—that's somewhere between an extremely dark, overcast day (100 lux) and regular workaday office lighting (320 lux).

Aside from the special considerations of oil paintings, take basic commonsense care with where you place your artwork. If you have wide, west-facing windows that give the room lots of strong afternoon sunlight (or east-facing windows that do the same in the morning), take care where you place your art. Also take into account the weather. We noticed artworks (and book covers!) fading a lot more in Oakland, California, where a west-facing apartment received almost uninterrupted sunlight, than in similar situation on the east coast, where weather is more varied. It's not that more diversely varied light doesn't damage your artwork, it just takes longer to do so. There is no way to protect your artwork 100 percent, just as there is no way to ensure the preservation of anything—as a famed geologist once noted to the writer Jonathan McPhee: "Given enough time, the life expectancy for everything is zero."

But we can take reasonable measures that our artworks outlast us, at the very least. For antique or fragile items, don't skimp on UV-resistant glazing, and always ensure, no matter what you're framing, to protect against acids in mats and frames.

A bright and cheery kitchen and the periodic table of the elements. *Christine Schmidt and Evan Gross, San Francisco, CA.*

RESOURCES AND FURTHER READING

We've always considered *How to Hang a Picture* more of an inspirational guidebook than a decor manual, and more of a reference guide than a detailed instruction book. We wanted to give the quick and essential facts about this curious little intersection of the art world with your day-to-day life. And since it is such a rich little intersection, there's always more to learn. While the best advice and insights we discovered came from asking experts and artists, there are plenty of resources, both online and printed, that can further inspire your explorations.

Essential Tools and Supplies

Framing tape
> **Utrecht Pro Framers Tape**
> www.utrecht.com

Picture hangers, wires, and hooks
> OOK brand picture hangers are reliable and easy to find in any hardware store or art supply shop. Our favorites include their conventional Zinc Hangers, Padded Professional Picture Hangers, Concrete and Brick Hangers, and Brick Hanging Clips. They also make wire, D rings, plate hangers, and other hanging essentials. www.ooks.com

Foamboard hangers
> **Foamfast Hangers** by Moore, available at most art supply shops

Foamboard is readily available at any art supply store. We don't have any particular brand recommendation—just make sure that what you buy is acid-free.

Frames
> Quality preconstructed frames can be found at
> > Crate and Barrel: www.crateandbarrel.com
> > Pottery Barn: www.potterybarn.com
> > Restoration Hardware: www.restorationhardware.com/

> If you're buying smaller-sized frames, Utrecht Art Supplies has affordable options: www.utrechtart.com

Mat boards
> Most mat board available at respectable art supply shops will be acid-free and acceptable for most framing needs. Strathmore museum-grade boards are 100 percent cotton and acid-free: www.strathmoreartist.com

Premade picture ledges
> IKEA's Ribba picture ledge is affordable and versatile: www.ikea.com
> Restoration Hardware sells different types of picture ledges in wood, glass, and stainless steel: www.restorationhardware.com

Hanging systems

AS Hanging Systems produces art-display systems and picture-hanging rails with a sleek steel design: www.ashanging.com

Other, nonessential tools

Point driver

An expensive tool, but useful if you're often lowering wood-stretched canvas paintings into frames. Logan makes point drivers with varying prices and functions: www.logangraphic.com

Kreg Jig

Not necessarily a starter tool—it's the kind of thing you get after you already own a table saw and a power drill and a jigsaw. It will, however, help turn a novice woodworker into a DIY powerhouse: www.kregtool.com

Fasteners and anchors

As we've said, our experience with fasteners has been that they are kind of like toothpaste—it's hard to tell a difference in quality between brands. Any brand you buy at a well-stocked hardware store should work just as well as another. Part of this is personal preference—you'll get to know which ones you like better the more you use them.

Style and Design Inspiration

Discussing style can always be difficult, because, well, style changes over time. That's why in this book we aimed to stay away from decor fashions and trends and stick to certain aesthetic principles that won't ebb and flow as much. That said, there's obviously a place for staying abreast of fashions and trends, especially when planning a wall display. Some of the best places to do this are online, where style blogs and art retailers can showcase the best and brightest designs and ideas from professionals and stylish enthusiasts.

Anthology Magazine. This beautifully produced print magazine offers shelter and lifestyle content, as well as a blog with more inspiration: www.anthologymag.com

Apartment Therapy. The classic go-to source for all kinds of real-life design solutions for the home and beyond: www.apartmenttherapy.com

Bloesem. Beautiful modern interiors curated with an appreciation for the hand-made and vintage details: www.bloesem.blogs.com

Cup of Jo. A lifestyle blog based in New York whose Home and Design section often features knock-out interiors: joannagoddard.blogspot.com/

Decor8. Internationally influential home decor site features beautiful and unusual interiors from around the world: decor8blog.com

Design*Sponge. Veterans of home decor and DYI projects online, Design*Sponge offers endless inspiration and easy how-tos: www.designsponge.com (See the book below)

Freunde von Freunden. An international interview magazine based in Berlin which aims to portray "people of diverse creative and cultural backgrounds in their homes and within their daily working environments." Their interiors march to the their own beat, often with surprising and unsual design solutions for hanging art: www.freundevonfreunden.com

Remodelista. A modern home decor, architecture, DYI and design Web site with a strong artisitic sensibility. They often feature innovative use of materials and design solutions: remodelista.com

We couldn't possibly list all the great home decor Web sites out there, but here's a few more worth visiting: **Adore Home Magazine** (www.adoremagazine.com), **Bright Bazaar** (www.brightbazaarblog.com), **The Design Files** (thedesignfiles.net), **Desire to Inspire** (www.desiretoinspire.net), **Fresh Home** (freshome.com), **The Inspired Room** (theinspiredroom.net), **Justina Blakeney** (blog.justinablakeney.com), **Sacramento Street** (www.sacramentostreet.com), **Simply Grove** (www.simplygrove.com) and **SFGirlbytheBay** (www.sfgirlbybay.com)

In book form:

Maxwell Gillingham-Ryan, *Apartment Therapy's Big Book of Small, Cool Spaces* (Clarkson Potter, 2010)

Meg Mateo Ilasco, *Crafting a Meaningful Home* (STC Craft, 2010)

Holly Becker and Joana Copestick, *Decorate: 1,000 professional design ideas for every room in your home* (Chronicle Books, 2011)

Holly Becker, *Decorate Workshop* (Chronicle Books, 2012)

Grace Boney, *Design*Sponge at Home* (Artisa, 2011)

Deborah Needleman, Sara Ruffin Costello, and Dana Caponigro, *Domino: The Book of Decorating.* (Simon & Schuster, 2008)

Deborah Needleman, *The Perfectly Imperfect Home* (Clarkson Potter, 2011)

Susan Bartlett Crater and Libby Cameron, *Sister Parish Design: On Decorating* (St. Martin's, 2009)

Christine Lemieux, *Undecorate* (Clarkson Potter, 2011)

How To and DIY Resources

Any of the big tomelike home-improvement bibles out there covers most of what we discuss in this section of the book—all about affixing heavy objects to drywall and making repairs and using tools. The problem with those big books is that they cover such broad topics that they need to assume a certain starting point of proficiency, which can be a problem when all you really want to know is how to use an anchor in your drywall. While we relied on local hardware store salespeople and general contractor friends to answer lots of our questions (as you should as well), we did find that there were a few small and approachable books that had great information about basic home repair and maintenance.

Earl Proulx's Yankee Home Hints (St. Martin's, 1993)

Arianne Cohen, *Help, It's Broken: A Fix-It Bible for the Repair-Impaired* (Filipacchi, 2011)

Martha Stewart's Homekeeping Handbook: The Essential Guide to Caring for Everything in Your Home (Clarkson Potter, 2006)

Mounting and Self-Framing Resources

Online resources for inspiration are plentiful, but are often short on details, so for a comprehensive overview of the science of mounting and framing artwork, it's best to utilize one of the many detailed books on the subject. Even if you don't plan on doing half of the work or buying the costly tools these books often prescribe, they are generally written by experts and will cover all the details on this very challenging subject. However, it's best to supplement any information you get from a book with the personal know-how of a professional. Run your ideas past a professional framer, develop relationships, ask questions!

David Logan, *Mat, Mount, and Frame It Yourself* (Watson-Guptill, 2002)

Kenn Oberrecht, *Home Book of Picture Framing* (Stackpole, 1998)

INDEX

ACKNOWLEDGMENTS

This book exists because of the kindness, goodwill, and expertise of many people, and while we're philosophically opposed to overly long acknowledgment pages, our gratitude compels us to say thanks where thanks are most certainly due. So, thank you: Joy Tutela at David Black Agency for guiding us with good cheer and wit, and to BJ Berti, Jasmine Faustino, and Kerri Resnick at St. Martin's Press—your book-building skills are top-notch; we salute you.

And to all the folks who gave us advice and information, shared art-hanging stories, and let us use their homes as inspiration for the watercolors in this book, we are supremely grateful: Rosanna Albertini, Esao Andrews, Claire Barliant, Lena Corwin, Jim Campbell, Lisa Congdon, Jenny Daugherty and Joe Conway, Ben and Laura DeHaan, Chelsea and Noah DeLorme, Miranda Dempster and Gus McKay, Lisa Ellsworth, Jordan and Paul Ferney, Susie Ghahremani, Sean Greene, Cat and Dan Grishaver, the staff at Maine Hardware in Portland, Maine, Tomer Hanuka, Luke Hoverman, Lisa Wong Jackson and Nick Jackson, Chrissa and Daniel Jalkut, James Jean, Stephen Kanner, Kate Lacey, Anh-Minh Le, Carol LeFlufy, Tara Mangini and Percy Bright, Meg Mateo-Ilasco, Sean McCarthy, Michael Morris, Alex Eben Meyer, Linda and John Meyers, Kristin Morrison, Neil O'Brien, Youngna Park and Jacob Krupnick, Marcia Prentice, Jordan Provost and Jason Wong, Sasha Ritter, Beth Salvini, Christine Schmidt and Evan Gross, Lorena Siminovich, Wendy and Scott Thorpe, Nicola Trezzi, Steven Wade, Olivia Warnecke, Anna Wolf and Mike Perry, and the staff at Zero Station Framers in Portland, Maine.

And finally, I'd like to thank my co-author, art director, and all-around design visionary, Suzanne LaGasa, for the nudges, both gentle and otherwise, that kept us on the path.